# Our Generation: *How America's culture has been fundamentally altered forever.*

By Cory Compton

# Foreword

Have you ever witnessed something, either on TV or in real life and you think to yourself, *"I know how this can be solved"*? Ever since my childhood years, I have constantly remained up-to-date on current events-specifically the more political and controversial ones. The stories I see on TV and from the people around me have enticed me to form these 'theories' on how to solve certain national problems. We've all had this spark of seemingly original ideas, and for me it was no different. My interest in politics sparked when I decided to put these theories into practice; to implement them. Yet it's impossible to remember every finite detail about these theories when your brain is the only storage unit you utilize; this is where this book comes into play.

Writing a book was the first idea that came to mind when I was considering the different options on how to record my theories. Finally, I can now highlight our national dilemmas and how to solve them. This isn't to say that my theories are the best; in fact, the book more centers on simply exposing our national troubles, while providing seemingly simple solutions. Too many people in this nation believe that everything is fine, but my hope and dream is that more people, after reading this book, will be experiencing a new level of alertness; alertness that everything *isn't* ok in this nation. If more people are aware of these problems, then naturally more theories and plausible solutions will generate as a result.

Truthfully and honestly, I believe that our nation is heading down a dangerous path. For the past few decades, we have gradually abandoned our traditional ideals in favor of more international ones. We are quickly losing our identity on work ethic, morals, independence, fair treatment, and economic structure. Perhaps this is easier for me to proclaim given my conservative values, but this book, while largely centering on conservative solutions, is worth a read by every belief on the political spectrum. For instance, in Chapter 4 I address the liberal indoctrination of our youth on college campuses. But this catastrophe, in my opinion, is more harmful to liberal youth than to conservative youth. When no dissenting opinions are forcing you to further investigate your own beliefs, or are there to challenge and force you to properly defend your opinions, then ultimately you will have a distorted view on life. You will not be prepared to face reality, where everyone's beliefs are subject to often-severe criticism. The national dilemmas I highlight affect everyone negatively, not just conservatives, which is why everyone should at least give this book a chance.

I do understand, however, that my book is amongst hundreds of my kind. Evidence-based books are nothing new, and are becoming increasingly popular. From Rand Paul's *Government Bullies* to David Bossie's *Hillary: The Politics of Personal Destruction* (Both of which I own), the competition is anything but equal. My book was never intended to compete against such giants; books written by famous politicians, White House staff, and talk-show hosts. I'm just a teenage white boy from Northern Michigan, what should I expect? That's exactly what makes this book stand out from the others; it's not the content of the book, but rather the author who wrote it. I'm 18 years old, and I started writing this book when I was 16. This kind of book being written by a teenager is virtually unheard of, and so I hope and pray that the older generations will look upon our youth in a new light. Millennials are notoriously (And sometimes justifiably) viewed as being stupid, ignorant, and entitled. This isn't always true; not every young person is a gullible progressive, and I pray that this book helps in justifying that claim.

I wish for more youth to be brought out of the darkness of ignorance; after all, we are the future of this nation. Given my age and status, my hope is that those qualities will entice more of our youth to read this book. Humans are geared to pay more attention to those of their own status; females are more likely to listen to other females; coaches are more likely to listen to other coaches; Republicans and Democrats are more likely to listen to others aligned to their beliefs, and this is no exception with youth. Younger people are more likely to pay attention to their own. I believe that the importance of this book would not be nearly as great if I were to write this later in life. I needed to write this while I was still young, so that this book doesn't simply get thrown into the steaming pile of similar books while still attempting to sing its own tune. *Our Generation* may not be the most exciting work you ever read, or even the most informative. My level of detail is nowhere close as detailed as the books written by the politicians, and it isn't supposed to be. The purpose is to educate others on the issues that our nation faces in a straightforward manner. I learned a lot on my journey while writing this book, and I'm sure you will too.

*Thank you for your interest.*

# Table of Contents:

## *Chapter 1*: Introduction

Nearly every single individual, sometime in their early existence, has been obligated to endure the pretentious rantings of either a grandparent or relative. The infamous "back when I was a kid" explanation has been repeated for generations, and while your grandparents proclaim it, chances are their grandparents repeated those exact same words to them when they were adolescents. But what's the explanation for it? Generally it means that society has been altered so thoroughly that it's at the point of being virtually unrecognizable compared to life 40-50 years ago. At least, that's the way Gramps always portrayed it to be. In the past, society has always experienced lenient progress at best; economically, socially, and technologically. So in the past, Gramps had little to bicker about, as his life was slightly different at best.

The landscape has changed now; within the last 20 years society has experienced an unprecedented leap in change, *especially* in the area of technology and politics. *Everyone* over the age of 25 has witnessed the entire American landscape change right before their eyes. Modern grandparents finally now have a legitimate excuse for their relentless bickering. This time everything *has* drastically changed compared to their lives, as this book later proves. Don't confuse this analogy as a scapegoat for me to ridicule the elderly, or to generalize them as being "stuck in the past". No, while I realize and accept that a large portion of this change has overall bettered our society, I realize that many, *many* important subjects have been either eliminated or negatively interpreted. Two steps forward, three steps back. This is what "progress" has succumbed to be called. This is the bar which has been set.

Perhaps this thought process truly differentiates me from the majority of my peers, and that largely bothers me, for rather it seems that most my age fail to pay attention, or oftentimes even care about what occurs in the world around them. For the modern era has affected more than just our outside universe; it has manipulated our minds, thoughts, and general actions as well. Since the 60's, the media has largely influenced how we as a society "are supposed to behave" and what we "are supposed to believe", and unfortunately a large portion of us have fallen into this trap (this will be covered more extensively in a later chapter). Other major factors include the invasion of technology, disappearing traditions, and an overall massive push for a more progressive culture.

Counter arguments may include ideas such as "how can this be possible if conservative presidents keep getting elected?" Having a traditionalist, conservative, or in other words non-progressive president in the oval office truly does little to alter the path this nation has endured for the past 15 years. It started when George W. Bush was in his early candidacy, and yet he is a Republican. As this book details, it's not the president that influences society; in reality they have little control over it. The media, in a more exclusionary scale, is the culprit. Again, much of this change is largely beneficial, such as greater diversity and tolerance (to an extent) towards others, especially on gay marriage. More cures for various illnesses are being discovered, technology has connected us on a scale only imaginable in science fiction, and new efforts are being presented to combat pollution. So to assume it is all negative is simply ignorance of the facts, yet a well-rounded individual should know both the positives and the negatives.

We extensively hear about how great everything seems to be, but this book addresses the issues most people may not ever consider, and it underlines how a well-rounded society should incorporate elements from both the past, and the present. Everyone knows the saying "If it ain't broke, don't fix it", yet it seems society has not, or rather ignores it. "Age old" concepts such as hard work, being a gentlemen to women (now considered sexist), and attempting to become independent are ideas that seem to be demonized in our culture. Some ideas, laws and regulations had to be changed for society to move forward, most notably in the areas of racial separation and discrimination against minority groups. There is a modern influx of attempting to change just about everything, whether justifiable or not, to encompass the idea of progress. The term is often misinterpreted, as progress isn't about changing or altering a concept just because it's old, but rather evaluating what should or shouldn't be changed to meet the requirements of modern society. The idea simply boils down to this; some things ought to be changed, some should not, as long as the older ideas have worked effectively in the past.

Unfortunately modern culture has failed to abide by this idea, in a vigorous attempt to "easternize" the United States to follow more closely to European nations, even though the main reason for the separation of America and Europe was largely due to our differences in how a country should operate. Until recently, stringent differences between them have always remained obvious; from the US containing the world's largest gun ownership rates compared to many European nations banning firearms altogether, to American football vs football (soccer). The US has always taken pride in being unique and standing out from other countries, yet now American culture, as viewed by a large portion of the world, is now considered not "up-to-date" to everyone else, especially reflecting upon our "gun culture". This is another reason for the push to manipulate our culture, to feel *accepted* by the others. Yet aren't these unique qualities the reason how the US managed to propel itself to become the main world superpower, in less than 500 years? I often speculate if the same people who demand consistent change ask themselves this very question.

This is the point that this book attempts to get across, how all of this sudden, rampant push for change may not be as beneficial as the government claims it is. We are going to be discussing a wide variety of topics, in significant detail, of how destructive certain changes can be. Of how and why certain ideas and concepts should always be a fraction of our society, of how quickly and rapidly changes have been brought upon, often due to redundant reasoning. But mostly, it is about an economic, cultural and technological shift in our nation that has caused a large, often unknown, dire consequence upon our lives. It doesn't matter if you're a Democrat or Republican, an atheist or religious individual, everyone should have the right to know the real reasoning behind certain actions, and I sincerely hope that a new point of view is presented, and a new thought to emerge, for people to think among themselves and consider "Is this really the direction we should be taking?" Because the truth is, while many of the changes have been beneficial, much of it has launched a full frontal assault on the very foundations that has kept our nation thriving.

## Chapter 2: Age of Technology

Out of all the major changes our world has experienced, perhaps the most noticeable piece is in the technological field. Technology has invaded and implemented itself within the fabric of society; controlling us, changing us, and altering our perspective view of the world. Gone are the days of eyeballing a map to figure out where to go, gone are the days when the CD case was browsed through to find the right album to play in the car, and gone are the moments of traveling to the local library to obtain information about a certain subject. VHS tapes have been replaced with DVDs, which were then replaced with Blue Ray, which is now being replaced with all-digital programs such as Netflix, all in just a little over 10 years.

This is not coincidental, yet astonishingly a mathematical certainty. Technology advances at such a rapid rate due to a formula known as *Moore's Law*. Discovered by Intel co-founder Gordon Moore in 1965, Moore observed that the number of transistors per square inch on integrated circuits had doubled every year since their invention. This essentially claims that the overall powers of technological machinery will double every year. At first the idea was laughable, Moore was sharply criticized due to his new formula, yet surprisingly enough history supports his claims to the fullest extent. This trend of doubling technological power has remained true and steady for the past 50 years, and has continued this way up until the 21st century, which is still to this day doubling every 18 months.[5/12]

This undoubtedly leads up to the next question: Where is the evidence which supports this theory? The proof is all around us; in fact most of our modern smartphones are far more powerful than even the most glamorous supercomputers 20 years ago. A single Apple iPhone 5 has 2.7 times the processing power than the 1985 Cray-2 supercomputer, which was *the* world's fastest computer from 1985-1989. The iconic gaming platform of the early 80's, the NES, contains half of the processing power as the computer that brought Apollo to the moon.[3] Yet perhaps the most incredible example is that a single chip inside a musical birthday card contains more computing power than the entire Allied forces in WWII.[4] The amount of exponential progress in the technological field clearly appears to be far surpassing virtually every other area in modern society. If any one aspect were to encompass our current generation, it would most certainly be technology.

To present just how far computing technology has come within the past few decades, consider the following: In 1993, the world's fastest supercomputer was the *Connection Machine*, running at 131 gigaflops. Today, the new record holder is China's *Tianhe-2*, running at 54.9 petaflops, which is 419,000x more powerful. The amount of processing power that the *Tianhe-2* wields is almost incomprehensible. For a computer to operate just a single petaflop, it must be able to perform 1 trillion calculations per second, over twice as many calculations per second as there are stars in the Milky Way Galaxy.[4] And what's even more incredible is that this behemoth of a machine will soon be surpassed by yet another supercomputer that is expected to be 20x faster than the *Tianhe-2*. President Obama has announced the construction of this new computer, set to go online by 2025, will attempt to achieve 1 *exaflop*, or 1,000 petaflops. Industry Tap, an engineering and trade publication, says that such a computer could be used to solve "some of today's great challenges, like more accurately modeling the Himalayan watershed, understanding how hurricanes form, determining how genes work on the molecular level and understanding how brain synapses work, [all of which] will require vastly more computing power than is currently available."[7] These new supercomputers hold a massive amount of potential opportunity, and if utilized properly, could greatly impact the progression of society. Indeed *Moore's Law* has and will continue to withstand the test of time.

Technology has advanced to the point where we are now able to manipulate the inner-workings of biology. Cloning is a relatively new invention; the first successful clone being the production of genetically identical mice. Today, several mammalian species have been cloned, including dogs, cattle, cats, rabbits, and even monkeys. The fact that we have successfully cloned a rhesus monkey is indicative as to how far cloning technology has come. Cloning humans and primates is considerably more difficult; spindle proteins, which are vital for reproduction, are much closer together in primate egg chromosomes than in other species.[16] Cloning extinct organisms is also a rising possibility. Movies like *Jurassic Park* are fictitious, but the possibilities of us achieving such feats are steadily increasing. Professor Hwang Woo-Suk, a South Korean cloning expert who is working closely with Russian experts, told The Siberian Times: "As a result of tireless joint efforts, we have achieved what we call the 'initial stage' on our way to recovering the mammoth."[15] Therefore, the possibility of recreating extinct life is becoming reality.

Yet this entire technological prowess can accumulate several unintended consequences as well. In short, new and improved gadgets are enticing and often addictive. In fact, 64% of American adults now own a smartphone of some kind, up from 35% in the spring of 2011. Unsurprisingly, the majority of smartphone users are young adults; 85% own at least one smartphone.[8] It goes far beyond smartphone consumption however, as modern technology influences nearly every portion of our 1st world lives. From the alarm going off in the morning, to turning on the TV to watch the weather forecast, to plugging in the auxiliary cord to play some favorite tunes on the way to school or work; we as a society are heavily dependent on technology. And it's seeping into some unexpected crevices as well. Several 2015 Chevrolet vehicles now contain 4G LTE Wi-Fi, there's the *iRobot* which will sweep your own floors so you won't have to, and even Walmart cashiers are being rapidly replaced with more "efficient" automated transferring systems. Coming to the realization, one could note how eerily similar our lives are transforming to mimic the movie *Wall-E*.

Speaking of Walmart cashiers, this leads to a whole new crisis to deal with. Across the nation, once human-exclusive jobs are gradually being replaced with machines. Realistically, robots replacing cashiers is most certainly expected, due to the job not being very complex and mostly dealing with mathematical problems, it appears to be the ideal location for a machine. The unfortunate truth however, is that new evidence suggests that machines will soon be replacing jobs that seemingly only humans could undergo.

According to NBC, pharmaceutical applications are already experiencing a new influx of machines. The UCSF Medical Center recently launched an automated, robotics-controlled pharmacy at 2 UCSF hospitals. Google has revealed plans to design automated cars which would replace taxi drivers. "Our automated cars, manned by trained operators, just drove from our Mountain View campus to our Santa Monica office and onto Hollywood Boulevard," said Google engineer Sebastian Thrun. "They've driven down Lombard Street, crossed the Golden Gate bridge, navigated the Pacific Coast Highway, and even made it all the way around Lake Tahoe." The extension further grasps other areas as well. Through a partnership with GM, NASA's *Robonaut 2* will soon be replacing astronauts in the areas of maintenance of space stations, but will projected to be assisting in scientific work in the near future as well. Currently it's even gone as far as babysitting children. NEC's *PaPeRo* robot has the ability to tell jokes, give quizzes, and track kids using a radio-frequency identification chip.[9] Businesses are quickly coming to the realization that machines can, and will be far more efficient than human labor. One can only speculate over the economic consequences that this presents, when the human workforce slowly disintegrates.

From an early age we are exposed to technology; as babies and toddlers we quickly realize that we become addicted to technology. *Elmo, Dora the Explorer*, and other educational programs are used right from the beginning to teach babies about proper behavior and basic math. In the past, parents never had the opportunity to rely on technology to perform a large portion of their parental jobs; instead they actually had to *teach* their kids themselves. Currently, several families are relying solely on technology to teach their children, which sounds odd, but keep in mind that doing this is a far easier alternative than doing it themselves. In fact, according to a recent study by San Francisco-based Common Sense Media, 38% of babies under 2 use tablets or smartphones, up from 10% in 2011.[1] Unfortunately, these generate an apocalypse of over dependency on electronic devices, yet in the eyes of society such effects are often encouraged rather than criticized. Just take a scroll through the app store; there is a multitudinous array of baby apps for just about every single area in the world of child bearing. Some fear technology could one day replace parental guidance entirely; in fact, there are already electronic nannies.

The consequences are already accumulating at an alarming rate. Due to the early introductions into the electronic universe, 1 in 11 children between the ages of 8 and 18 years already have technology addictions. So approximately 9% of American kids are addicted to their devices, main culprit being the over dependency on technology for teaching purposes. Not only that, but parents' technological addictions are lessening their chances of interacting with their kids. Studies show that one in three parents prefer using technology to playing with their child.[10] This indicates that the addictive attitudes do not just include children, but rather humanity as a whole. Smartphones, tablets, and personal computers are loaded with new and improved features, businesses and corporations intentionally design these devices like this to attract customers, and the method works remarkably well.

Such a cultural addiction has generated unique results; the creation of completely-new brain disorders. According to the results of one UK survey, 73% of participants experienced unusually high amounts of panic upon misplacing their phone, and for another 14%, the panic turned to desperation. This phenomenon has resulted in the formation of Nomophobia-an official disorder added in 2012. Others include Technoference-technology interfering with our personal lives. In one 2014 study, more than half of the 143 participants said that tech devices interrupt their leisure time, conversations, and meals with their significant other. And then there's the mysterious Phantom Ring-the perception that one's device is vibrating, when in fact, it's not. David Laramie, a clinical psychologist in Los Angeles, polled 320 adult mobile phone users, in which two-thirds of them reported experiencing phantom ringing. But perhaps the most frightening one is what's known as the Truman Show Delusion-named after the 1998 film *The Truman Show*, where the main character feels like he's being watched, which turned out to be correct.[14] Due to material we are exposed to on a constant basis; ideas of being under constant surveillance has been popularized with organizations such as the NSA, CIA, and FBI. Combine that with cameras basically equipped on every new gadget, and the result is the delusion that one feels like they are always being watched.

Technology can either be beneficial or harmful depending on how it's utilized, it's a beast that must be tamed, or else it shall devour all that steps in its path. If the creature is not tamed, it will break free and ensue chaos upon our lives; clinging to us and never releasing, demanding our constant attention, and absorbing our very lives into its own form to further spread its influence, and it has already begun. According to Nielsen's Total Audience Report, Americans aged 18 and older spend more than 11 hours a day watching TV, listening to the radio or using smartphones and other electronic devices.[2] However, if technology is domesticated, it wields the potential to perform the bidding of mankind, and we can manipulate its power for the progression of humanity, bending its will to align itself with ours. The difficulty is to find a balance; an equilibrium to how much technology should truly be a part of our lives. If we grant technology too much of a presence, we become slaves, developing an uncontrollable addiction like meth heads to our electronic devices. As Henry David Thoreau proclaims: "Men have become the tools of their tools." Poor guy must be rolling in his grave right now.

Why do we allow ourselves to be so thoroughly engrossed in technology, why is this addiction so obnoxiously difficult to overcome? Like drugs, technology makes us "feel" good, using it as a scapegoat to avoid the stresses of life, which are remarkably similar reasons for getting stoned. Maybe we ought to outlaw electronic devices 'cause it's basically heroin on a screen. Social media champions the notion that it allows us to connect easier with other human beings, yet face-to-face communication has been on the decline in recent years. In a 2012 study, families who reported spending less time with one another increased from 8% in 2000 to 32% in 2011.[11] Technology is frequently used as a method of diverting contact away with other people, and it works well, I've done it more than a few times. But doing this discourages the idea of engaging in meaningful conversations with others, and in several cases has gotten to the point where speaking in person creates an atmosphere of awkwardness. The one area where humanity should always refrain from allowing technology to seep in is in our instinctive, naturally born behavior. Mankind has survived thus far due to the ability to communicate, to be able to exchange information, and removing that from our nature is like removing the talons from an eagle, all the while claiming that the eagle is fine.

Humanity has become so entrenched into technology that our species would simply deteriorate if it were to disappear. The world as we know it would plunge into eternal chaos, so we remain heavily reliant on electricity, machines, and our gadgets to continue stabilizing society. Overall however, one could easily argue how technology has allowed us to advance the human race on an unprecedented scale. Modern science, medicine, construction, internet, power, and everything in between are all the effects of technological prowess and advancement; nobody could possibly refute its importance in our world. What we must always be continually aware and cautionary of is the possibility of technology taking control of our lives. In many cases, it's already reality, but this is an issue that will only escalate in the future as technology further advances and gains more traction in our lives.

If *Moore's Law* and other laws such as *Kryder's Law* (doubling of storage space every year) persists, then in the next 2 decades our technological capabilities could be up to a *million* times greater than now; in 3 decades a *billion*, 4 decades a *trillion*, and in 5 decades a *quadrillion* times greater, that is if the laws continue to remain true.[12/13] If it seems unbelievable, then do the math. If our current year begins at 1, then next year it will be 2, year after 4, then

8, then 16 and so on; continue the doubling process until it's been repeated 20 times, and you will conclude with 1,048,576 - which is how many times more powerful technology will become compared with our current abilities. Most current adolescence, *our generation*, will witness the greatest influx of change in our world, greater than all the rest in mankind's history combined. 30-40 years from now, technology may become so wildly advanced that we would be able to develop machines that have the ability to upgrade and improve *themselves*, both living and nonliving particles would be colonizing and inhabiting every corner of the solar system and beyond, we could generate entire ecosystems, and computers would be implemented into our minds, thoughts, and actions, because we as humans would simply be incapable of recognizing the fierce rate of technological improvement without the assistance of artificial intelligence. This is why zombie movies never bother me, but films like *The Terminator* frighten me to an extent, because such a scenario could *very easily* occur.

But when does it end? Is there an eventual limit to technological expansion, and if so, when would we reach it? As of now, this is not an answerable question, and won't be for some time. A possibility to consider is that eventually human colonization will reach other planets, perhaps other solar systems and maybe other galaxies. New, complex resources may be discovered, and the process can restart all over again. The only limitation on technological advancement isn't in the process itself, but rather our incapabilities of being human. If we design self-upgradable robots, *they* could end up being the ones to invent new technologies rather than humans, yet the frightening aspect to this is that one day technology may control *us* rather than us being in charge. These may all seem like nothing more than philosophical pondering, but they are all very highly in the realm of possibilities. Technology holds the power to make or break the human race, which is why it's so imperative that humans remain in control.

Technology is a train, an army, a force too great and too powerful to conquer. There is not a single other area that has progressed *nearly* as fast as technology, nothing comes even remotely close. Technology engulfs us, dazzles us, constrains us, and sets our minds free. It is the wondrous inventor of modern civilization, and the great destroyer of all of humanity. We cannot understand or even attempt to comprehend it, so we just go along with "magic". It is absolutely amazing how such complex works of technological creations were derived from this planet, originally from raw materials, from discovering fire to inventing virtual reality, and humans have not been around for very long. We all wait in anticipation for what the future holds; we all hold our breaths and cross our fingers, all waiting for the day that all of our wildest imaginations will become true, and simultaneously losing our humanity inch by inch without even realizing it. There's no doubt, no wonder, no speculation in that we, *our generation*, are about to embark on the craziest journey in all of mankind. If our Grandparents complained about all the change they've witnessed in their lives, just *wait* and see how we're going to act after we've seen it all, the difference won't even compare.

Technology has taken over to begin a lifetime rule over the people, like a king inheriting the throne. It is captivating, mesmerizing, independent, and most importantly, it can be controlling and manipulative. The unparalleled escalation and ferocious advancement of technology is nearly blinding, in what is now considered to be the greatest factor and area of influence on our entire lives. Our tools are not dependent on us to utilize them; we have instead become dependent on them to solve our greatest problems. Either through the good or the bad, nobody can deny the vast magnitude of the presence that technology has upon us. It is no surprise now that the 21st century will forever be known as the Age of Technology.

# *Chapter 3*: Political Correctness

First and foremost, what does the term "Political Correctness" even mean? Is it nothing more than a derogatory analysis imagined by the Tea Party, or is it actually dangerous with the stark similarities it holds with the censoring of free speech? Political Correctness, or "PC" for short, is a term describing how multiple statements, words, and actions are either highly criticized, altogether avoided, or manipulated that are perceived to ridicule groups of people who are either disadvantaged or discriminated against. In other words, any form of expression that would, in any way, appear offensive or intolerant against any particular group of people; whether it be race, gender, or religion, is completely avoided. While on paper this may appear to be a reasonable concept; truthfully it can be a danger to Democracy. The issues begin almost immediately, such as who decides what would be considered intolerant behavior? Would this include ALL groups of people, even those that may hold the majority of the population? (Many studies show that this is frequently not the case). Will this concept violate certain Constitutional rights? And how far would this concept be taken? Numerous forms of what would be considered innocent expression could be deemed "intolerant" by extremists in any faction; even though realistically these actions would, by any rational person, be perfectly tolerable.

Going back to my previous statement, how is being PC a menace to Democracy? The answer is simple; it completely violates many of our 1st Amendment rights, such as freedom of speech. Making this claim is understandably controversial, there's nothing wrong with the promotion of tolerance and equality, however, the current trends outlining our PC culture is anything but promoting true, fair treatment. One of the essential facts about life is this: No matter who you are, what you believe, or what race you may be, you will experience things that will offend you, that will make your blood boil, and this is something we must all accept. The key is how to deal with such situations, containing a strong mind is essential in progressing through life. Collapsing in an emotional breakdown whenever hearing a different opinion will create a massive struggle in staying happy and stable through life. Unfortunately, modern society fails to comprehend this, and instead campaigns censorship to avoid the possibility of being offensive. This rigid censorship can cause catastrophic consequences, and could accelerate the very problems PC was supposed to vanquish.

These problems are vital discussions that cannot take place in an extremely PC culture. More sensitive discussions regarding race, gender, beliefs etc. are now more frequently being avoided, because people are unable to voice their opinions without being labeled a "racist", "bigot", "sexist", etc. as these accusations are reputation killers. So if these crucial topics are being avoided, it is now becoming more increasingly difficult to resolve these issues, therefore inhibiting progress. It is impossible to exchange ideas and information if certain opinions are shutout entirely. In fact, the use of words such as racist, sexist, homophobic and the like are misused or misinterpreted repeatedly. For example, if a Christian claims to not agree with homosexual marriage, does that mean he/she is a homophobe? To some people, the answer is an indefinite yes; however, factually it's absolutely not homophobic. Disagreeing with a movement does not equate to the despising or fear of those affiliated with it, which is what homophobia truly means; the fear of homosexuals. Little do some realize, but labeling someone a sexist or a racist is a massive accusation, which is why they are known for demolishing, even without evidence, a lifetime of positive accomplishments-they can ruin people's lives.

Yet most of these statements are laughed off by a good portion of people. Political Correctness is controversial in the sense that its supporters proclaim it to be nothing more than showing tolerance towards others, and that the Right has simply twisted it for their own exploitations. While occasionally that may be the case, overall the PC culture has in several instances gone too extreme, to the point where some of our rights as citizens of the United States are being infringed upon. As Dr. Ben Carson explains "Political Correctness is antithetical to our founding principles of freedom of speech and freedom of expression. Its most powerful tool is intimidation." The intimidation being conformity, conforming to think and behave the way society wants us to. This is the core of the Politically Correct, to disable and exile others' opinions to further enhance their own ideologies.

The most notable areas where Political Correctness has run amuck are at college campuses. Take for instance an incident in Santa Cruz, California, where Stevenson College was forced to apologize for serving Mexican cuisine at an alien-themed event. The administration received numerous complaints from students declaring a connection between the food and "illegal aliens", therefore incoherently making the incident racist, according to them. Carolyn Golz, a student life administrator, later announced "As a result of this incident, I will require cultural competence training for Programs staff, in addition to implementing mechanisms for future program planning that will ensure college programs are culturally sensitive and inclusive."[4] To summarize this, an unintentional "mistake" was branded racist by a group of severely sensitive students who are unable to grow a pair. The amount of irony in this situation is nearly traumatizing, the students themselves had to make the correlation between Mexicans and illegal aliens, meaning *they* stereotypically compared the two. Wouldn't such outlandish assumptions in fact brand the *accusers* as behaving in a racist manner? This is yet another hazard associated with the PC police, hypocrisy being a major offensive.

Yet another politically correct tragedy occurred in, you guessed it, California. The University of California has recently purged several phrases that could *potentially* be deemed "offensive". Students are encouraged to avoid statements such as: "America is a melting pot," "Why are you so quiet?" and "I believe the most qualified person should get the job." To claim the reasoning for these statements as ridiculous would most certainly be an understatement. Saying, "There is only one race, the human race," is offensive because it denies "the significance of a person of color's racial/ethnic experience and history." Claiming "America is the land of opportunity," implies that "People of color are lazy and/or incompetent and need to work harder." And asking an Asian, Latino, or Native American "why are you so quiet?" is associated to giving the order "assimilate to dominant culture."[5] Yet again hypocrisy is at the root of these idiotic proclamations, drawing stereotypical assumptions for racist accusations does nothing positive in *actually* combating *real* racism or sexism. Race baiting is a dangerous tactic, as more often than not it stirs racially charged environments, rather than repelling it. The issue with implementing Political Correctness in colleges is simple; in these 'safe places', students fail to gain experience which will assist them in the real world. The real world cares very little about sensitive emotions and hurt feelings, 'safe places' just don't exist outside the classrooms.

It would most certainly be a dream come to life if the spread of Political Correctness never seeped outside of college campuses. Unfortunately this is not the case, as PC culture has rooted itself in the media as well. This is *very* dangerous, as media is highly influential in our lives. Some news corporations have become a politically correct spawning ground, such as Al Jazeera English. Al Jazeera has been known for leaning obnoxiously far left in its ideologies; in 2015 they released a YouTube video on July 4th which labeled America as being obese, violent, and racist.[9] This time the hypocritical side of Political Correctness has once again reared its ugly face; while Al Jazeera argues free speech to criticize the United States, they want to limit those same protections when they are veered towards Islam and terrorism. Al Jazeera English executive Carlos van Meek banned his news employees from using words like "terrorist," "Islamist" and "jihad". The reasoning? For terrorism he writes "One person's terrorist is another person's freedom fight". He also retorts "Do not use Islamist" because it's "a simplistic label." And don't use "jihad," he said, because "strictly speaking, jihad means an inner spiritual struggle, not a holy war. It is not by tradition a negative term. It also means the struggle to defend Islam against things challenging it." He instead urged his employees to use words such as "fighters" and "militants" as replacement terminology.[8] Whenever terrorism strikes; whether it be on 9/11, the Boston Bombings, San Bernardino, or the Paris attacks, such attacks should *always* be labeled for what it is. To refer terrorists as simply "militants" disregards them as a credible threat, it undermines the very real impact they play in the destruction of world peace.

There's a reason why I am highly critical of Political Correctness, it's because this phenomenon has hit close to home for me. There are multiple things that I dislike about my school; terrible food, lack of extracurricular activities, lack of career advancement opportunities, etc. However, the one thing that I've always enjoyed about it was our uniqueness in sports. The Chiefs, with the black and orange color scheme and the iconic chief-head logo; it has defined us for years. I'd always feel a sense of pride running onto the football field when I was younger, knowing that our mascot was way cooler than the other team's. That logo was respected and revered by all, and boosted our morale knowing that we can handle tough situations; because we were *Chiefs*. Then it all changed: In 2013, a complaint was filed by the Michigan Department of Civil Rights with the United States Department of Education, Office of Civil Rights, asking the federal agency to issue an order prohibiting the use of Native American mascots, names, nicknames, slogans, and imagery.[10] Our logo officially transformed from a detailed, mesmerizing chieftain face, into a "C" with a chief headdress on top. This new change infuriated a good portion of the students (including me), and for good reason; either way, we were powerless to do anything about it. The pride, the comradery, the morale; all appeared to vanish in this new era of PC culture. The new icon now holds little value compared with the original, it's difficult now to walk onto the football field with the same intensity, knowing that you're now defending a "C", not a mighty chieftain warrior, but a simplistic "C". It's just not the same experience anymore.

The entire concept of Political Correctness is little more than a tactic used to strip away our first amendment liberties. Americans notice and understand this; and thus many are infuriated over it, rightfully so. This is why individuals such as Donald Trump and Ben Carson have accumulated so much momentum with voters; their popularity (more so with Trump) stems from the idea of being as politically incorrect as possible. If this violation of rights were not such a major issue at this moment, Trump's plans of banning Muslims or strengthening immigration policies would've most likely have been negated and disenfranchised. Candidates exploit and take advantage of this anger that has recently been sweeping across the nation, but there are problems with this. When people allow this anger to control their thoughts and actions, this often leads to disruptive thinking. Many Conservatives support Trump's plan of banning Muslims-largely due to the fact that the plan is a massive middle-finger to the PC culture, something very few people have been publically willing to accomplish. In reality this idea is extremely dangerous, and possibly unconstitutional; something that any Conservative should be up in arms over.

The Constitution's "bar against declaring an official religion" would apply to discrimination against non-citizens, argues Harvard law professor Laurence Tribe.[11] Even if the proposal was for security and the prevention of terrorist activity within our nation, the effects could very well be the complete opposite. A 51-minute propaganda video released by al-Shabaab, al-Qaeda's Somalia-based affiliate, included a scene in which Donald Trump states "Donald J. Trump is calling for a total and complete shutdown of Muslims entering the United States until our country's representatives can figure out what the [expletive] is going on." (They bleep out the word "hell" in the video).[12] This suggests that Trump's plan on preserving our safety is instead being backfired as a terrorist recruitment tool. Despite all this, his popularity among his base has only risen, due to a massive factor; it is politically incorrect. Such extreme statements would've leveled any other candidate, but because the anger against the PC culture is so great, people are willing to tolerate more irrational concepts to degrade Political Correctness.

The entirety of Political Correctness is atrocious; the enforcement to silence opinions for the sake of clarity is a recipe for disaster. It is the unwillingness to engage in critical discussions due to the potential of collapsing one's reputation or career. The truth becomes silenced, facts are deemed offensive, and statistics are pushed under the rug; if the government views them as discriminatory. It is no wonder that Americans-who have enjoyed freely expressing themselves in the past, are now outraged at this now embraced ideology. When the president himself fails to address terrorism as *radical Islamic* terrorism, then we most certainly have a problematic situation on our hands. If the American people don't stand up against this violation of human rights, it will only escalate from here. While this may appear to be an issue which is dismissed by Liberals and embraced by Conservatives, in actuality all of us should be, at the very minimum, upset with how extreme this once logical idea has become. Being politically correct does *not* make you correct, and being offended does *not* make you right. Nobody's voice should be silenced, and the first amendment is what has allowed us to express our individuality. This is a right in which we all adhere to, and it is the American duty to defend this, even against our own government. Political Correctness is nothing more than tyranny with a friendly gesture. It must not be allowed to expand any further, to intimidate and berate us anymore. The truth always prevails; logic and facts will always defeat emotions and being "offended". It is our right to express ourselves to our preferences, and this right should always be preserved.

## *Chapter 4*: The Indoctrination

One of the many fantastic opportunities with the United States is the freedom to openly express ourselves. We have the right to individualize ourselves and to differentiate ourselves from any particular area in society. Not only do we have the right to do that, but due to our cultural influences, the thought has been ingrained in us so that we *strive* to accomplish uniqueness; Americans prefer to stand out from the crowd due to our individualistic society. It appears foolish or outrageous to us that some people would prefer conforming to a group rather than expressing their individualism. This is in fact, how the majority of the world operates. Eastern culture emphasizes collectivism; that every person is simply contributing to a larger cause. They strengthen the concept that everyone and everything is intricately connected, that individualizing oneself is foolishness and unnecessary. Being a highly outspoken individual who would rather cram my opinions down the throats of others, I feel very fortunate to be living in the Western hemisphere.

Free thought and free expression does carry its load of consequences however; according to the circumstance, certain opinions can shutout others, alienating those who have believed in those ideas. While we may be a nation of individualism, human nature tells us to try to be socially accepted; sometimes this means sacrificing the urge to express one's own ideas for the sake of belonging. If we say or do anything that may eliminate our presence in a group, club, school, or organization, then we tend to divert those ideas and continue saying what is acceptable in that particular group. There is always the danger of accidentally isolating oneself for expressing oneself; this is where peer pressure comes in. Either through threat or temptation; directly or indirectly, our peers indulge as a major influence on our thinking processes. When the majority opinion dominates a certain region, the minority opinion is casted away; and less and less people continue supporting the minority opinion. This can either be positive or negative, depending on the situation. Historically, slowly but surely, more reasonable ideologies have shutout the previous irrational ones; from slavery to equal rights to scientific advances, this plays as a major factor in the progression of society.

Recently this trend has accumulated into a significant hazard; as the shutting out of opinions has transferred from individuals themselves, to so-called objective organizations; such as news and public education. There's nothing immoral with expressing oneself-it's the leakage of bias propaganda into areas where the curriculum demands objective behavior. In the past, common sense and rational thought allowed moral ideologies to flourish, brainwashing techniques aren't necessary if the hatchling opinion can be agreed upon by any sane human being. What's occurring now isn't the push for common-sense ideas; in fact it's the push for highly controversial or divisive ones; such as abortion or gun control, where strong opinions exist on both sides. However due to peer pressure and conformity; these otherwise controversial opinions are being more accepted while the other side of the spectrum is being cast away. And not only are some opinions being ignored, they're often being *demonized* along with its supporters. Where did it come from? How did it begin? When did this start? The answers for all of these are broad and shady at best; all it requires is a single outspoken idea to take root before it spreads like wildfire. A celebrity's or a journalist's opinion will receive far more recognition than anything that a common civilian presents, and this will assist tremendously in the spread of information.

The silencing of certain opinions sounds awful close to Political Correctness, and it is. The difference between Political Correctness and what's been recently occurring is that while Political Correctness focuses primarily on incorporating a censorship on certain actions or sayings, what's now happening is the *replacement* of the silenced opinions, a *push* for a new agenda. I like to refer to this phenomenon as the *Indoctrination*. When the majority of the media and college curriculums are under the influence of a single political branch of ideologies, severe consequences are inevitably within the near future. Through the influence of these, slowly but surely the minds of the American people could also sway to the side as the media. The concept has been distilled that progressive ideology is the 'only' way to move our country forward, and that the other side of the spectrum is 'stuck in the past' due to traditionalist values. That's the concept that both colleges and the media have incoherently adopted.

As referenced in the previous chapter, colleges have transformed into 'safe spaces' where nobody's feelings are allowed to be damaged. A major culprit for this could be the recent spike in Liberal professors and a recent decrease in both Conservative and moderate ones. In 2014, roughly 60 percent of professors identified as "liberal" or "far left," according to the Higher Education Research Institute at UCLA, which was reported by The Washington Post's

"Wonkblog". When that data is compared with a similar survey from 1990, only 42 percent said the same. Combine this with the dwindling population of Conservatives and moderates teaching at universities; the number of professors who identified as "conservative" or "far right" during the same time span dropped by nearly 6 percent, while the amount of "moderate" professors fell by 13 percent. This therefore leaves those who identify as Conservative to be at a little over 10 percent, those who pertain to be moderate at just under 30 percent, and those who identify as Liberal at 60 percent.[2] This has generated a tremendous gap between the different political ideologies at a 5:1 ratio. With the lack of diversity of opinions among college campuses, Conservative and moderate students are continually bombarded with criticism and ridicule for possessing their beliefs; their opinions being challenged on a daily basis. This can in fact be beneficial for these students; they are exposed to different points of view and can expand their horizons because of it. Having a good understanding of both sides of an issue is essential in the development of a healthy, intellectual mind. Indeed, the ones who truly suffer from this calamity are Liberal students, whether they realize it or not. Instead of being presented with new ways of thinking to challenge their thought processes, their opinions are simply reinforced. They get no exposure, no real-world experience, and by the time they leave college, they will have this idea ingrained into them that everyone holds the same viewpoints as them.

Conservative students often leave college with a more Liberal focus, and already Liberal students sway even farther to the left. This is why colleges have been dubbed as a spawning ground for Liberalism, because everyone comes out reallocated a little farther to the left (Generally speaking, congrats to those who leave unscathed in their viewpoints). It appears that nobody truly benefits from this occurrence; Conservatives are being pressured to change, and Liberals are never challenged with new ways of thinking. In fact one of the only people who truly benefit from this is, unsurprisingly, Democratic politicians. "47 professors at the top 50 liberal arts colleges in the country, as ranked by U.S. News & World Report, have given to presidential campaigns, according to donations recorded in the third quarter by the Federal Election Commission and aggregated by Campus Reform, a conservative watchdog of higher education". History professor Robert Paquet from Hamilton College was the only one to donate to a Republican-$150 to Carly Fiorina's campaign. Mr. Paquet later told Campus Reform that he was the "only out-of-closet conservative in a faculty of 200." Also according to Campus Reform from a 2012 study; 96 percent of Ivy League donations went to the Obama campaign, and currently 95 percent have given to the Democratic candidates.[1] This further reinforces the highly prevalent bias that is emerging in America's campuses, with one area completely dominating all other viewpoints; an intrusive situation that signifies the barbaric policies of many of America's institutions.

The United States has always been known as a biological melting pot; a combination of every racial and religious group worldwide. This has been due to our tantamount in promoting freedom and equal opportunity, which has therefore attracted individuals from every corner of the globe who are searching for a more sustainable life. This diversity in race, beliefs, opinions, and culture has made us strong and highly influential, with ample opportunity to be able to locate others with similar preferences as oneself. Our unification lies within our differences, yet this becomes greatly threatened when diversity begins to fade away, *especially* when correlating to education. The effects of decreasing diversity in the classroom stems far beyond the notion of simply not being subject to different ways of thinking; it's a full frontal assault on the structural integrity that has made this nation flourish, the foundations which has defined us as a nation where all are welcome and accepted. A slow but thorough process, eliminating certain opinions in colleges will ultimately eradicate those opinions from ever emerging again in those locations. That is, unless more students can remain firm in their beliefs; which is vastly different than being 'intolerant' or 'close-minded', because at this point, it means not succumbing to *brainwashing*. A less politically correct term I like to use to describe this current catastrophe; anytime people are only presented with one side to any story, by a supposedly *objective* environment that is paid for with public funds in order to further advance their own agenda, it is most *certainly* a tactic of brainwashing. And why would one suppose that this data goes unreported by the majority of the public media? The answer is simple; they believe and support the same agenda that colleges promote, for a similar situation has been occurring in the news room.

The US media is the largest source in which the American populace obtains their information from. CNN, ABC, CBS, NBC, PBS, and FOX; the largest news stations, are corporate giants that are very selective in what they wish their audience to view, and five of them are eerily similar to one another in their biased affiliations. The first five listed possess left-wing favorability, and are biased against Republicans. In fact, Fox News is the *only* major news source that has a right-wing bias rather than being skewed to the left, which might explain why the station receives so much negativity from the Liberal population. We've all heard about Liberal media bias, yet very few of us actually take these accusations into thoughtful consideration. I'll be rather blunt about it; Liberal bias is *real*, and it is a threat to quality journalism, to any credible analysis of the world in which we inhabit, we have to trust that the information we receive ought to be verifiable, accurate, and overall objective, which is simply false in the modern era.

Let's analyze media bias into different categories: Donations, Political Beliefs, and Coverage. When we look at campaign donations under the microscope, we notice a very distinct bias towards Democratic candidates; In a 2008 survey of 144 journalists nationwide, they were 8 times more likely to make campaign contributions to Democrats than to Republicans. On top of that, a 2008 *Investor's Business Daily* study put the campaign donation ratio at 11.5-to-1, with a Democratic favoring. In terms of total cash given, the ratio was 15-to-1; in terms of actual dollars donated in 2008, the Democratic Party received a total donation of $1,020,816 from 1,160 employees of the three major news media outlets, while the Republican Party only received $142,863 from 193 donors.[4] There may have been substantial, energetic enthusiasm for Barack Obama's election, but the imbalance is still far too high to be accounted as reasonable.

Now let's take a gander at the political beliefs of the media. In fact, slanted media bias has always been prevalent, and been a pressing issue since the 60's, when In 1964, 94% of media professionals voted for Democrat Lyndon Johnson over Republican Barry Goldwater. So media bias is nothing new, nothing unusual, and nothing extraordinary; however, only recently has this bias been exposed. A high favorability of the Democratic candidate over any Republican incumbent has stayed consistent since then; such as In 1980, when twice as many casted support for Jimmy Carter rather than for Ronald Reagan. And when it boiled down to party affiliations, a 2014 study by Indiana University's School of Journalism found that just 7.1% of all journalists identified themselves as Republicans, vs 28.1% who self-identified as Democrats and 50.2% who said they were Independents. Then there are the actual beliefs of the news media on specific issues. 81% of news journalists favor affirmative action in employment and education, 71% agree that the "government should work to ensure that everyone has a job", and 75% believe that the "government should work to reduce the income gap between rich and poor."[4] To summarize, the vast majority of news journalists support the candidate, have similar beliefs as, and self-identify with the Democratic Party.

Investigating the actual coverage of the news media is the most crucial component of the entire analysis; in truth it doesn't really matter what the political beliefs of the media are, what truly matters is if they apply these beliefs to skew the news. Unfortunately, the news is often altered to align with their politics. The Pew Research Center's Project for Excellence in Journalism released a report in 2012 over the coverage of President Obama and incumbent Mitt Romney. They both received roughly equal amounts of coverage, but the kind of coverage was vastly different; In evening news for example, narratives of Obama remained balanced, while the negative exceeded the positive by 17 percent for Romney, and the coverage of Romney was also twice as negative as that of President Obama-23 percent vs 11 percent. Another interesting notion is that while Fox News is constantly bombarded for being too biased; and this may be true to an extent, 46 percent of coverage for the president was negative in 2012, it actually pales in comparison with MSNBC during the same election, where coverage of Romney was 71 percent negative. The appalling bias of MSNBC didn't stop there, during the final week of the election, MSNBC presented no negative coverage of President Obama and no positive coverage of Governor Romney.[3] This therefore concluded to be the greatest absolute bias offered by any of the primary news outlets; it's a real shame that MSNBC never gets scrutinized as frequently as Fox News, despite apparently harboring even more biased favorability.

Conservative values have long since been alienated from America's newsrooms and college campuses, and these two applications are both *highly* influential in US politics. Not only does this diminish the opportunity to expand one's own horizons by an exposition to new concepts and thought processes, it also completely undermines democratic diversity and the representation of certain ideological beliefs. It's a massive blow to what journalism is supposed to stand for, and it's a menace to a supportive educational system where supposedly everyone gets equal representation. This stems far past the unfair criticizing and targeting of a political party, for those are rights in itself; to be allowed to question other's opinions. This instead is a promotion for anti-American values-*Communist* values, where one is not allowed to believe in certain ways. That is what we like to refer as the indoctrination; a consecutive, formulated strategy in the advancement of one ideology over another. What's occurring are not regular actions that the United States proceeds in, it's the manipulative process of fundamentally transforming our culture; and when you have complete control over the very news that the civilian populace watches, the process is much easier. It may not seem like a particularly massive ordeal that the news and colleges are slanted; one could argue that this is simply one of the possible negatives of freedom of speech and expression. This is true, and would be acceptable if said news outlets and colleges would be more open with their real views, instead of hiding and pretending to be truthful and objective, because that's what we like to refer to as *lying*.

We are a nation of diversity, a nation that prides itself in our differences and our ability to openly express our differences. When selected viewpoints and people are unjustly targeted for the sake of advancing one's own agenda, you're not just targeting a viewpoint; you're targeting democratic values and responsibilities. If any of these slanted opinions derived from private institutions, there would be no issue; however when verified, public, government owned institutions show slanted ideologies, then that shows clear favoritism of one viewpoint over another, and it is dangerous in the tranquility of this nation, where everyone should feel like their views are well-represented and hold some sort of an influence. When this is combined with the other nationwide atrocity known as Political Correctness, an unstoppable force of brainwashing and indoctrinating others sweeps through these great lands. We are a nation of individualism, of uniqueness, of non-conformity; not the other way around. These Constitutional rights should always be upheld and protected, and nobody should feel forced into conforming and changing their ideologies in the need to feel accepted.

## Chapter 5: Vanishing Traditions

"This is pointless, we're wasting our time." I whispered to my father on a chilling, cloudy evening on November 19, 2011. "My brother and my cousins already got theirs, and we haven't seen anything all day!" My father and I sat in the dark, confined space near a pond; looking, listening, anticipating any sort of movement. I glanced over at the decaying bolt-action .308 that was quietly resting against the rotting walls, itching to fire that old rifle on an unsuspecting target. He slowly yet assertively looked over at me, and with a commanding tone exclaimed "Patience. Your time will come, but you *must* be patient." The sentence fell upon deaf ears, my internal impatience and frustration consumed my entire well-being at this point; I felt as if God himself was giving me the cold shoulder. I squinted my eyes, narrowing my focus on the semi-open field 100 yards in front of us, scanning the terrain for any forms of life. Nothing but the quiet stillness of the trees was all that befell upon my vision. Nobody warned me that hunting would be this despicable.

It was the fourth day of rifle season, on opening day the majority of my peers have already snatched their bucks-all spikers. Despite the relatively small deer that nonetheless protruded intense pride from them, I grew immensely jealous over them; crossing my arms in solitude as my brother and cousins were getting pictures taken of them standing next to their respective trophies, large smiles radiating from all of them-4 in total. It was the only subject that I could think about on this quiet November evening, as hope was quickly fading about my possibility of obtaining my own prize; that was, until my dad made the startling announcement of "Look!". My face instantly rose, making an attempt on seeing whatever it was that he saw, yet found nothing. "You're looking in the wrong direction" he proclaimed, pointing his finger at a conglomerate of bushes in the left corner of the field. I narrowed my vision once more, and this time I actually did see something, though it was rather difficult to pinpoint what it was. I witnessed a white blur behind the brush, and that's when I finally realized what it was.

*Antlers*. Instantly my heartbeat accelerated, and my mind in a rapid flurry of confusion and excitement. My father made a minute hint towards my right, in which I slowly clenched my hands around the rifle at my side and cautiously raised it; setting the barrel so that the tip is just barely creeping over the edge of the window. I tightened the firearm into my shoulder, and peeked through the scope at the white object that hides behind the forest walls. It was indeed a rack; the size still unknown unless it were to present itself into a more identifiable view-which it did. The figure scampered to the right, a head extending out of the thicket. My heart rate exponentially increased yet again, this time It beat so viciously that it was the only sound that I could hear; it overpowered all the other noises of the forest. Not only was it a rack, but a *big* one; I estimated it to be around a six to an eight point. Once I said this to my father, he remained in his calm stature, yet again whispering "Wait". This was extremely difficult for me to accomplish; my entire body at this point was trembling in anxiety and extraordinary excitement, as I kept my sights on the deer. It appeared to notice our mixed bait of corn, beets, apples, and carrots and slowly progressed towards the food; the entire body in plain view. I knew at this moment that this would be my only opportunity to strike.

"Shoot just behind the front thighs, breathe slowly and fire halfway when you're exhaling." I tried to listen to these orders; breathing in long, heavy strides in an attempt to slow my heart rate, which didn't work. However it did increase my focus; I hastily turned the safety off, and carefully rested my finger on the trigger of the wooden rifle. During these exhilarating moments-this moment in particular, will forever elapse as the most gut-wrenching moment of my life thus far. It is during these events that one feels as if the stars themselves have aligned to make this possible; so many things that could go wrong, so many variables to consider, and one mistake could spell doom upon the entire opportunity. What if the deer runs away? What if I miss? What if the bullet accidentally nicks a branch or twig which would set it off-course? If I miss, would I get another chance as this one? What if I hit it and end up being unable to locate it? All these thoughts fluctuating through my mind, but at this moment I had to expel them, and focus on just one variable; getting the kill.

My ears rang, unable to even notice the gunshot through the excitement. I could not comprehend what was occurring around me, until I looked out and noticed something that caused my heart to hit the floor. The deer was *gone*, and instantly those previous questions re-emerged into my mind. "It ran into the woods, just north of us." My father stated, seemingly unaffected by the entire situation. "Do you think I shot it?" I remarked, hoping for a reassuring reply. Once again that same response bubbled up "We'll just have to wait and see." So we waited, in what felt like the longest wait of my entire existence; the same questions floating around in my thoughts. My dad rest his feet on the opening of the blind, and pulled out a cigarette from his pocket. "You always have a smoke after taking a shot." He proclaimed, with a voice now at normal volume. "So how'd you think you did?" He chuckled, with a grin on his face. I was mesmerized, why would he be happy if he doesn't even know I got the kill? "It's not over yet!" I barked, in an attempt to denounce my father to hold the same stresses as me. "Don't worry, I heard a crash. You got that buck "

After fifteen excruciating minutes, we went out of the blind and came upon the spot of where the deer stood. He pointed at the ground, and gleaming off the reflection of his flashlight-was blood. We followed the blood trail until we came upon a body leaning against the side of a pine, and there I saw it, a large, beautiful eight point with its bloody tongue extending out in a sign of defeat. All the fears, all the worries, all the variables, immediately vanished. Out of all the emotions encircling me when lifting up the deer's heavy antlers, surprisingly enough the most prominent one, was a feeling of relief. Out of all the possibilities of failure, none of them came to pass, and looking back I understand just how enormously fortunate I was. Nothing else that I've experienced; whether it be my first job interview, my first time performing in a talent show, or even my first relationship, could compare to the emotional anxiety of shooting that very first buck, and the sheer joy and pride of sitting on that corpse and smiling towards the camera.

These are the kinds of experiences that have taught me valuable lessons; patience, maturity, humility, calmness, and the list goes on. It's these moments that remain ingrained into your memory for the rest of your life; perfect stories to address around the campfire. Hunting is an amazing experience; the adrenaline rush and nervousness that accumulates when eyeing a large buck within the crosshairs supersedes any other similarly intense moment of my life; because one knows how fortunate they are when coming across such an opportunity. There's only one shot, and there may not be a second chance; some hunt their whole lives yet never get the chance to strike. But every year they still try, every year they believe it will be their year; despite their luck in the past. That's the beauty of hunting. It provides hope time and time again for a chance to obtain glory. It allows us to unleash our instinctive will to hunt which has allowed us to survive for thousands of years. And for those that still do it, there's only one word which can describe this continual will. It's simply *tradition*.

The unfortunate reality of the situation now, is that generational traditions such as hunting are dwindling. As more people migrate into the cities (2.3 million more in 2013 than 2012), less are occupying country and small town residencies.[1] This in turn leaves a great void in rural communities which is unable to be filled. Hunting in particular has been hit hard with this trend; statistics from the U.S. Fish and Wildlife Service show that the number of hunters 16 and older declined by 10 percent between 1996 and 2006 - from 14 million to about 12.5 million. It has since then continued to decline at a rapid rate; along with fishing - a 15 percent decrease from 1996 - 2006.[2] Simply less people are willing to contribute the time or energy into obtaining their own food and would rather purchase it at the grocery store. If the decline continues at this rate, then in a few decades virtually nobody will be hunting or fishing; the traditions gone.

Another major tradition that has been on a violent decrease is the American family. The standard American dream has always been a family with a mother and father and children. Soon however, that idea will be a rare exception rather than the normal situation. Citing a Pew Research Center report, The Deseret News notes that the U.S. marriage rate has steadily dropped by generation from 65 percent of the Silent Generation (1960) to 48 percent of the Baby Boomer Generation (1980) to 36 percent of the Gen X Generation (1997), to just 26 percent of the Millennial Generation (2013).[3] The traditional value of marriage has disintegrated; the millennial generation simply is not the kind that is generally able to commit to a lifelong partnership. These are usually values passed down through families about the importance of marriage, yet just like with recreational hunting; the traditions fail to be taught and practiced and in turn slowly die out. Upon that point there is little that can be accomplished which can bring it back to life.

Some traditions had to be destroyed for our nation to progress; racism and sexism being among the largest culprits. However some teach us valuable life lessons that encompass moral activities; they teach us to be a better person. These traditions are just one of many culprits of this nationwide movement to change virtually everything; whether good or bad, to reflect upon the misconceived idea of progress. As stated in the first chapter, progress is not simply the transformation of everything deemed old; It is evaluating both the positive and negative aspects of history and deciding which ideas should remain and which should, for the betterment of everyone, be crushed. Historical traditions tend to lean towards ideas of hard work and commitment, and the current entitlement generation would rather lean towards the simplistic and easy ideas. The two simply cannot mix without an external interference.

The concept boils down to this; I may have had the luxury to tell my own hunting tale, but memories like it will soon be a part of the past. These stories will be replaced with stories of how many likes on Facebook one got, or instances of being able to hide the weed from the cops when getting pulled over. Those memories teach nothing about lifelong moral values; but instead elaborate on selfishness, greed, and being an 'effective' criminal. Hunting has taught me to be patient; waiting hours, perhaps days for the kill to arrive. It has taught me how to be committed; traveling to the blind every morning at 5:30 and not leaving until the sun disappears from the horizon. But most importantly it taught me to be thankful; and to make the most of any opportunity that I come across. These are concepts that I can use to be successful. Sadly however, most in this era are unable to extract such values from their traditions, because they simply don't have any anymore. But all is not lost; perhaps new traditions can form from current families that teach lifelong skills and ideas, so that we can hold on to the moral values of the past.

## *Chapter 6*: Gun Control

The United States prides itself in believing that this nation is unique in areas such as freedom, equality, and justice. However, these concepts alone do not differentiate us from the rest of the developed world. Great Britain has freedom, France has equality, and Canada is just. Virtually all industrialized nations support these essential rights. We are not special due to those; what *truly* differentiates us is one specific right that has been eliminated in most developed countries, a right that has protected us from tyranny and oppression and has allowed our great nation to remain secure. Unfortunately, this right-along with so many other concepts are being threatened under the new idea of 'progress'. It has now been recently evaluated as being 'outdated' and faces the possibility of following suit to our European brethren in its ultimate elimination. And if that day arrives, we will be in severe danger.

This right is the 2nd Amendment: "A well- regulated militia, being necessary to the security of a free state, the right to keep and bear arms, shall not be infringed." We may share a multitude of the basic fundamental principles with the rest of the world, but our ability to own firearms is a right that others simply cannot enjoy; a right that allows us to put food on the table, to protect ourselves and our personal property, and most importantly, it allows us to keep our own government in check just in case it decides to manipulate our lives. It is a right, essentially, that has allowed all the other Constitutional rights the ability to exist. If the colonies' citizens didn't possess firearms during the American Revolution, then we would still be a colony of Great Britain; not an independent world superpower. That is how vitally important this amendment is, and why it is so vitally crucial to not undermine its importance, even in modern society.

Fortunately enough, the majority of Americans recognize and utilize the right to bear arms. In fact, we are by far the most armed nation on the globe-90 guns per 100 people; the second being Yemen with 55 guns per 100 people. This comprises 62 percent of the entire US population.[1] It has embedded itself as a fabric of our nation, a vital component in the functioning of the United States. The enterprise is so large that the amount of registered hunters from Michigan, Pennsylvania, Wisconsin, and West Virginia alone would be established as the world's largest standing army.[2] It would basically be suicide for any other country to attempt an invasion of the United States, *if* they somehow manage to repel our own military; with $682 billion in defense spending compared with a total of $652 billion with the next 10 most powerful countries.[3] It is essentially a double-layered firewall to repel against foreign invasion. We don't have to worry about that; what must be considered, however, are threats by our own government.

No single aspect of American society is protected against the onslaught of radical progressivism, including the 2nd amendment. It would appear to be a ridiculous concept, an illogical conspiracy theory to suggest that the feds are planning on confiscating all of our guns in one unconstitutional swipe; and realistically, that is most certainly true. There is no possible way that such actions would prevail without tremendous revolt, and most likely the overthrowing of our entire government for blatantly violating the very fundamentals of this nation. This doesn't, however, suggest that the eventual outlawing of firearms isn't the final goal of some individuals in power; I believe that is the dream for many of them. These are the same people who continually look towards Europe for guidance and ideas, and we all know what they've done about firearm ownership. They view the concept as inhumane and inconsistent with modern life, and that it shouldn't be a part of civilization for the violence commonly associated with guns. This is the conclusion that nations such as the UK, Japan, France, China, Australia, and dozens more have abided with.

The process to achieve this goal will not be in the form of one massive undertaking, but rather in a precise, seemingly unnoticeable process. It involves a circulation of demonizing gun lobbyists such as the NRA, using *pathos* during tragedies such as shootings and suicides to brand firearms in a negative light (Will we do nothing to protect the children?), increasing the difficulty for registration, and either limiting or banning certain pieces such as specific ammo types, magazine/clip capacities, and certain kinds of guns (Does anyone really need a .50 caliber?). It is a gradual, slow, decisive operation; the hopes that the combinations of all these will eventually persuade the average civilian to announce "Do we really need guns?" Because if at least the majority is enticed to believe this, then they'll elect those who will carry out the actions and the American gun owner soon finds themselves in severe danger.

There are already prominent figures of the left who are willing to cast blame on the NRA for gun related deaths. Take for example Hillary Clinton, who was willing to politicize the 2015 shooting at Umpqua Community College in Oregon. "It is infuriating. Every time there is another massacre, Republicans and the NRA, 'now is not the time to talk about guns.' Yes it is. But more than talk, it is time to act. But Republicans keep refusing to do anything to protect our communities. They put the NRA ahead of American families. It is wrong and we need to make every politician who sides with them to look into the eyes of parents whose children have been murdered and explain why they listen to the gun lobbyists instead." After the statement (and more was addressed) she received a thunderous applause. This is already the aspect of stage 1, the demonization process. She and others similar frequently politicize any and all mass shootings, declaring that 'something' must be done about guns. "It is wrong and we need to make every politician who sides with them to look into the eyes of parents whose children have been murdered and explain why they listen to the gun lobbyists instead." Clinton's last sentence of her statement; personally attacking Republicans and the NRA by casting them as child killers.[4] One would think that such statements cross the line in the professional world, but individuals like her use everything in their arsenal to enhance their support, even if that includes branding her opponents as essentially murderers; a seemingly effective tool in gaining support for the enforcement of more gun control.

However, Clinton has denied some key facts over mass shootings. According to the Crime Prevention Research Center (CPRC), 92% of mass shootings from January 2009 to July 2014 occurred in gun-free zones.[5] Yet she and her peers are devout advocates for increased gun control, perhaps Republicans and the NRA could use Hillary's own rhetoric against her? Popular phrases such as 'the only way to kill a bad guy with a gun is a good guy with a gun' and 'guns don't kill people, people kill people' appear to be awfully simplistic, yet data and statistics validate these claims; they hold truth. The data from the CPRC shouldn't be considered a surprise, when logic and reasoning is taken into account for why there are more shootings in gun-free areas. In a gun-free zone, the citizens in those areas are virtually defenseless against an attack. Nobody can stop the perpetrator other than by a suicidal charge or dialing the police, in which by then it is already too late. It's essentially the same thing as a thief infiltrating one's home and the owners possessing no way to defend themselves; easy pickings for the thief. If there were to be another who was also packing to act as retaliation, then the criminal could be stopped dead in their tracks before massacring innocents.

But Clinton may have the upper hand here; if she were to be president (which she may already be by the time this book is finished), then she will be presented with a perfect opportunity to pass her kinds of legislation. Due to Antonin Scalia's death and her ability to appoint new Supreme Court justices, the 2nd Amendment (among others) could be placed in jeopardy. For the first time in years, a Liberal majority would be the benefactor in legislative ruling; giving them the ultimate jurisdiction in laws. These new positions will have an everlasting effect on Supreme Court rulings in the United States due to lifetime memberships; and if it seems unlikely that she would attempt to undermine the right to bear arms, consider the fact that she believes Bernie Sanders is too soft on gun control. She would attempt everything in her power to achieve her goal of wrapping chains around the 2nd Amendment and choking the life out of it; once again part of the vigorous movement in progressive change.

The controversy covering gun control hits home on a personal level. With 14 registered firearms and counting, gun ownership and usage is extremely prevalent among my family. We, along with millions of other American citizens, possess these *tools* for various reasons: Hunting, protection, targeting shooting, historical items to be passed through the generations-in which the beauty of guns is their withstanding ability to survive and be used as long as they've been properly handled, makes them perfect gateways into witnessing, holding, and *using* historical artifacts. There was a paper I wrote back in my early Sophomore year in high school, one that still resonates and applies now more than previously due to this universal degradation of the right to bear arms. The short passage goes as follows, on October 30, 2014:

"Every day I wake up, I look outside the window and realize how fortunate I am, fortunate enough to live and contribute a part in the immense tranquility, sanctity, and prosperity of our great and flourishing nation, a nation that is unlike all the others. The United States truly is a success story, starting from the ground up. Starting out as a few hundred starving, ill, and weary puritans, and transforming into the most economically stable, most prosperous, and most powerful nation on earth in just a few short centuries; now ahead of countries thousands of years older than us. There is a reason for this; our Founding Fathers forged a constitution and a style of government unknown to the dominantly patriarchal world that they inhabited at the time. It was a new, intuitive, and dangerous concept, but as we've seen its progression throughout our history, it has proven to be a massive success. A government by the people, for the people. This is why we advanced so quickly, because our capitalistic, free-market society paved the way to be able to achieve the American Dream. The ability to accomplish one's aspirations, the ability to triumph over the seemingly impossible, the ability to have the freedom to do what you choose, and last but certainly not least, the ability to arm and protect oneself against the possibility of a tyrannical government, the basis for why the 2nd amendment was written. "A well-regulated militia, being necessary to the security of a free state, the right to keep and bear arms, shall not be infringed." - 2nd Amendment. Apparently, the term "Shall not be infringed" has been casted aside, or simply forgotten. As president John F. Kennedy once said: "Every citizen must be ready to participate in the defense of his country. For that reason I believe the Second Amendment will always be important." Even liberal presidents such as him recognized the importance of the 2nd amendment, so where is all this pushing for gun control coming from? Perhaps this next aphorism best applies to the situation that we are currently dealing with, with a government that is consistently increasing in size and in regulatory demands: "Americans have the right and advantages of being armed- unlike the citizens of the countries whose governments are afraid to trust the people with arms." - James Madison, *The Federalist Papers.* Such governments who are afraid to trust its citizens being armed are extremely prevalent in Europe, Asia, the Middle East, and now even Canada. As Adolf Hitler once said "To conquer a nation, first disarm its citizens." Fortunately for us however, we don't have a government of such a kind (yet), and we still have the freedom to protect ourselves from enemies, both domestically and overseas. There's more to firearm ownership than that though; the main reason is for self-defense (national survey showed 48% primary reason), but it's also for hunting (36%), target shooting (only 4%), decorative, concealed carry, or an item used to store old memories and traditions that are passed down throughout the generations. My Grandpa gave me a 1946 Savage 12-gauge for my birthday, whose dad passed it down to him 40 years ago. I cherish that firearm, not because I'm a deranged killer, but because it paints an era of days long past, and my memories of him will always be in the shape of that old gun. To the eyes of some, firearms are nothing more than tools used to wreak havoc and chaos, and should not be a part of modern society. But to the eyes of others, such as myself, they mean much, much more than just being an inanimate object. The moment I received that polished old cannon from the cold grip of my Grandpa's hands, I felt a sudden burst of anxiety and excitement, a kind of excitement that cannot be felt in any other way. A sense of pride knowing that you are holding a piece of history. The sad reality however, is that such special moments are vanishing from our society. The amount of active hunters has sharply declined (Michigan fell 31% in the past 20 years), and firearm ownership in general is currently in a downward spiral (49% owned in 1973, to just 34% in 2012). - GSS Survey. In short, American traditions are vanishing, and the United States that our Founding Fathers envisioned has morphed into something completely different. There is a reason why our nation is as prosperous as it is, because of our style and methods, but now it has been made clear that we simply are abandoning these methods. I want what made us great back, I want our values back, all the gun-totin', war mongering, hardy individuals that we once were. I want America back."

The passage may have been a tad intolerable in some areas, but the message remains truthful. The United States simply has materialized into a new entity; one that attempts to associate its beliefs with that of other nations, rather than pertaining to our interests alone. Our government has been systematically cornered by the rest of the world, in which they question and doubt our tactics on firearm ownership. This presents two choices for our officials; cave into the demands of European influence or remain firm with the American people. It appears they chose to cave in, leaving *us* to fend for ourselves. For the first time in history, gun owners nationwide are feeling fierce international and domestic pressure over their decisions.

But why would the possession of firearms cause such widespread controversy if the facts and statistics support our cause? In the book *The Bias Against Guns*, John R. Lott cites a 1986 survey in which 56 percent of felons across 10 state prisons said they would not attack a potential victim known to be armed, and also states that the "National Institute of Justice survey found that 74 percent of the convicts who had committed a burglary or violent crime agreed: 'One reason burglars avoid houses when people are at home is that they fear being shot'". Another aspect that demands investigation would be the current condition in locations with strict gun control. The infamous problematic situation in Chicago is cited often, and for good reason. The city has transitioned into the poster child for how gun control fails to work. The number of shootings in the city surged to 677 from 359 a year earlier. The city is on track to have more than 500 killings this year, which would make this just the third year since 2004 that Chicago topped that figure.[7] And

Chicago isn't the only place to experience this dilemma; Washington D.C., Detroit, and New Orleans are experiencing similar problems.

Not to mention that the whole concept of gun-free zones has virtually collapsed on itself here in the States. Along with the data mentioned earlier, the amount of shootings that occur in areas with the *least* amount of firearm restrictions and/or an area with a higher concentration of law-abiding gun owners are significantly lower. When was the last time you've heard of any mass shootings at locations with particularly high amounts of firearm circulation, such as gun shows? Aside from occasional accidental shots being fired; mass shootings are virtually non-existent at those places. Also worth addressing is that while Americans are purchasing more firearms (88.8 guns per 100 people in 2007 vs 84 per 100 in 2001), the overall frequency of gun-related crimes has decreased; the lowest rate since 1981 with 3.59 deaths per 100,000 people.[10] There is more to gun violence than the media wishes to broadcast, to say the least.

One of the primary arguments that gun control advocates incorporate is the correlation between gun violence in states with the gun laws of other 1st world nations such as Australia, Germany, and Canada. While there are facts which suggest that gun violence is lower in those areas due to extremely strict gun laws or the outright outlawing of guns, the whole story is never revealed. What is rarely taken into consideration is the *culture* of the other countries compared with ours. Geographical size, population, ethnical diversity, and most importantly the *history* of a country all play a role in the effectiveness of certain laws; particularly ones such as gun control, that involves an increased role in federal government.

Considering our large size, massive cultural diversity, and history of using guns to acquire independence from tyranny; assuming gun control will work here as well as the smaller countries that haven't had much of a history of gun ownership to *begin* with is certainly painting a picture that fails to tell the whole story. The reason why we are so adamant in keeping our guns is for a variety of reasons; mainly that we realize the importance of gun ownership because firearms arguably led to the creation of the United States, and that Europe and other nations worldwide have experienced atrocities due to an unarmed populace, such as the Nazi regime and Stalin, in which the threat of government tyranny is always prevalent, and we as a nation wish to always be prepared for such an occurrence if it were to commence again. It is *not* unrealistic to assume that a nation's government could turn tyrannical, considering the history of the human race. Perhaps it's because some of us don't want history to repeat itself.

Then there is the argument of the overall trustworthiness of those with CPL's. How do we know that they won't turn rabid? How can we infer that they'll make the right choices in case of an emergency? Worry not, for this is rarely an arising issue. Between May 2007 and March 2010, 9 law enforcement officers and 142 citizens were killed by concealed handgun permit holders-only .003% of all murders in that time frame. Generally, those with CPL's are trustworthy and reliable; they are also effective as a deterrent too. Citizens approximately kill twice as many criminals as the police yearly (1,527 to 606). Also, *Newsweek's* audience learned that "Only 2 percent of civilian shootings involved an innocent person mistakenly identified as a criminal. The 'error rate' for the police, however, was 11 percent, more than five times as high."[8] This doesn't impose that civilians are doing a better job than the police, for that is incorrect. The statistics do imply however, that when gun control proponents assume that the whole 'good guy with a gun saves the day' scenarios are nothing more than fairytales perpetrated by the NRA; they would be incorrect. This is exactly why criminals generally avoid confrontations with armed civilians.

And there are always other arguments, such as the ability to kill more people by using firearms. It would be common sense to assume that using a gun would clearly be more effective than a knife or a baseball bat, but on top of the ability for an armed populace to retaliate against the attacker; there are always alternative ways to commit mass slaughter. Were any guns involved with the September 11 attacks? Or how about more recently, when a terrorist killed over 80 people in Nice, France in a couple of minutes by using nothing more than a *truck*, and yet you don't hear of any legislation to control trucks or airplanes. Simply disarming the population does not deter mass killings, and there will always be other ways to initiate these killings without the need for firearms. The only difference now is that those who already illegally obtain their guns or whatever device they plan on using, they can be sure that the civilian population will be unable to defend themselves.

So what can we do about gun violence in America? If gun control fails to work efficiently, why not instead try the alternative solution? "The definition of insanity is repeating the same behaviors and expecting a different outcome" - Albert Einstein. Virtually every time there is a shooting, the only thing that is ever proposed is increased gun control; not mental illness, radical Islamic terrorism, or criminal history of the perpetrator. Even when all the mass shootings already occur in gun-free zones or locations with extremely high gun control, that is the only viable option which is presented, and time and time again it fails to work. The opposite occurs, actually, in that it generates more danger and more avenues for shootings. What our government is doing *is* insanity at this point, and it's past time to consider new solutions.

The first way we can minimize mass shootings would be to completely eradicate gun-free zones in public areas. The National Association of School Resource Officers cited a 2009 study that found the presence of school officers, who are sometimes armed, was attributable to a nearly 73 percent decrease in arrests involving possession of a weapon on school property.[9] The mere presence of an armed civilian deters criminal activity, so why prevent these deterrents from stepping foot in the most vulnerable spots for shootings? Another tactic that could be used, specifically in schools, would be to enact training sessions for students on how to repel an armed criminal by using charging methods to overpower the criminal, as mentioned before by Ben Carson. Some students may die, but the overall casualty rate would be far lower than if the students ran and hid. An increased vetting system for refugees would also reduce the effects of domestic terrorism with guns.

The 2nd Amendment is more than just an amendment; it is the foundation of the creation of the greatest nation in the world. It is a repellant against government tyranny, and allocates more power to the people. It's what differentiates us from the rest of the world, and overall that's fine with us, as they can continue to be defenseless subjects in a world where violence is on the rise.

Without this amendment, there would be no other amendments, let alone the United States itself. Gun control is nothing more than federal overreach and a scheme to acquire additional power, but unlike the situations of the past, we have the constitutional ability to fight back. It's ironic how we're pushing for more choice, equality and acceptance of other's beliefs and ideologies, yet apparently this excludes gun ownership. The ability to own guns is a right given to us by our Founding Fathers, not a privilege that the government can take away at any given point. This is why this right must always be preserved and defended, because we have learned from the past, and it is our duty to remember the millions who have suffered under tyranny. If history has taught us one important lesson, it's that you *never* allocate all the power to the government.

## *Chapter 7*: Prejudice: A Two-way Street

Humanity as a whole has always strived for the betterment and improvement of all of our lives, where the greater good prevails through revolution, sacrifice, or negotiation. Slowly but surely, tyrannical authority is overthrown, criminals are prosecuted, and civilians' lives are improved. Mankind has been a cyclical process of evil introducing itself and the power of good destroying it, whether it be the collapse of the Roman Empire, the defeat of the Nazis, or the domino effect of monarchical governments being transformed into democracies after the American Revolution. The stories and fairytales of good continually winning are, in many instances, seen as a fact throughout human history.

And yet the reality of the situation is far more complex. The end achievement for human equality has been progressing at a snail's pace since the dawn of time, and many of these still lingering problems should never have been issues to be addressed in the first place. Some of the biggest obstacles blocking the road to success is racism, sexism, and the overall unfair treatment of certain individuals through no fault of their own. Prejudice has blocked these people from enjoying life to the fullest; the color of their skin, their religion, sexual orientation, or sex transforming into curses upon them. The fact that prejudice exists epitomizes the harsh reality that mankind as a whole is extremely imperfect, and despite our achievements and advancements even in these areas, prejudice still exists and is alive and well throughout many locations in the world-including the United States.

I will not however, preach about how horribly minorities, homosexuals, and women are treated here in an attempt to ridicule the United States; those are common Liberal talking points, and in some instances, hold some validity, though in reality is far from true in general terms. Minorities, homosexuals, and women arguably are granted the best opportunities to be successful here more than anywhere else in the world. Then why do I bother mentioning the states as a harbor for prejudice then? What we instead suffer from, is a combatant against prejudice by injecting additional prejudice. This means that in order to give minorities additional benefits in society, we have cut many of those same opportunities to the Caucasian community. A prime example of modern prejudice would be affirmative action, where schools and colleges are obligated to enroll African Americans over whites, which in turn damages the other's chances due to the color of their skin. Racism includes Caucasians, believe it or not.

Everyone is familiar with Martin Luther King Jr.'s "I Have a Dream" speech, which includes the section "I have a dream that my four little children will one day live in a nation where they will not be judged by the color of their skin but by the content of their character."[1] Fifty-three years later, that dream still has failed to flourish. We *still* live in a society where people are, in fact, judged by the color of their skin rather than by their character and accomplishments. Undoubtedly, the treatment of African Americans in the states has advanced dramatically since MLK Jr.'s speech, an accomplishment that we can pride ourselves in as a nation, which is not the issue we face today. What we face today is the failure in recognizing the true nature of racism. Racism is *not* one-sided. It does not specifically target just African Americans, or Latinos, or Asians, it targets *everyone*.

History has proven this concept; all races have been slaves, all races have been slaveholders. From Chinese husbands enslaving their wives and daughters in 1000 AD, then they themselves becoming slaves to the Mongol empire in 1200 AD, to the enslavement of Hispanics by Spanish Conquistadors in the early 1500's, in which they became slaveholders during the mid-1800's.[6/8] Even white people were subject to slavery; an estimated 1 - 1.25 million European Christians were enslaved by African Muslims between 1530 and 1780.[3/4] African leaders even assisted Europeans during the Transatlantic Slave Trade by raiding other tribes and selling their own people for profit and munitions.[2] Slavery, therefore, was not originally perpetrated by any one race; it was a collective disaster that required collective unity to resolve. Today, the issue of slavery has transferred into the issue of discrimination.

In order to acquire the status of being a truly advanced society, one of the primary components is the complete elimination of prejudice of *any* kind. Nobody should be granted additional opportunities or a leg-up of any kind simply due to their race, which is rewarding people for something they have no control or influence over-essentially a participation trophy and an indirect form of discrimination. True equality involves constructing a system that rewards individuals via their accomplishments, character, and work ethic, rather than by gender or race. It also means promoting the intolerance of discrimination against anyone, not just minorities, and being able to view prejudice on an equal level and not prioritizing one form over another based on whomever is targeted. We have yet to accomplish this.

In 2005, during an interview with Mike Wallace on *60 Minutes*, Morgan Freeman perfectly depicted how a post-racial society should behave. During the interview, he claims that Black History Month is "ridiculous" because "Black History is American History". He also argues that in order to combat racism, we have to "Stop talking about it. I'm going to stop calling you a white man. And I'm going to ask you to stop calling me a black man. I know you as Mike Wallace. You know me as Morgan Freeman. You're not going to say, 'I know this white guy named Mike Wallace.' Hear what I'm saying?"[9] I hear what you are saying. You're saying that we need to stop categorizing people as being 'Black', 'White', 'Asian', or 'Hispanic'. That people should never be evaluated or judged based on race, that here in the United States, we are all simply Americans.

A seemingly unifying idea that, unfortunately, is completely discarded in many instances, and the irony is that modern-day discrimination exists to 'combat' racism. If every race has been subject to racism and slavery, then why is it that the black community has Black History Month, and whites do not? Why is it that organizations such as the NAACP and Black Entertainment Television (BET) exist yet the creation of any white duplicates would be categorized as 'racist' and immediately shutdown? Why is it perfectly acceptable to be proud of any racial heritage besides white? I'm certainly not advocating for the creation of 'White History Month' or 'White Entertainment Television' because they should not be necessary in a post-racial society, just like with BET and the NAACP. Any organization or event that encourages exclusion or separation based on race is arguably discriminatory, therefore detracting from the progress of unification. If the Miss Black American pageant only allows African Americans to contend, it is therefore discriminatory by excluding other races.

Many universities are following a similar example to what Georgetown University is enacting. In order to 'apologize' for the sale of 272 people in 1838 by two priests-who served as president of Georgetown, the University now gives slave descendants priority for admission, priority over standard ones.[10] Most of the time, the intention of such acts are positive, but in reality develop a negative outcome. Valuing the admission of one student over another due to ancestry is discrimination. Another, more shocking form of indirect racism can be extracted from a 2015 Princeton University study which analyzed how ethnicity affect admissions by using SAT scores as a benchmark. According to the study, African Americans received a bonus of 230 SAT points, for Hispanics an additional 185 points, none for Whites, and yet Asian Americans were penalized by 50 points.[11] The reason behind this is the same reasoning used to justify Affirmative Action, being, in quote from a 2003 Supreme Court ruling (which upheld the University of Michigan Law School's Affirmative Action plan) "Student body diversity is a compelling state interest that can justify the use of race in university admissions"[12] This means that the reasoning could be due to the greater Asian American population in colleges compared to other minorities (49% have a bachelor's degree, compared with 28% of the general population), therefore, projecting another futile attempt in diversification.[13]

Are we not a nation that advocates success through work, achievement through dedication, advancement through skill? The Asian American population is being penalized because they are 'too' successful, Affirmative Action does not apply to them because they are a 'Model Minority'. This implies that we are instead a nation that encourages success through heritage, achievement through ancestry, advancement through race. This form of indirect discrimination extends farther than discriminating against Asian Americans; it discriminates against the moral principles of this nation and completely undermines the traditional notion that success is only possible through hard work and determination. In Chapter 5 I mentioned national traditions that are deteriorating, one of them being the encouragement of a high work-ethic. The modern irony is that this rigorous diversification process is dividing this country; Asian Americans and Caucasians feel excluded whereas African Americans and Hispanics get the impression that the rest of us view them as 'needy', therefore making them feel insignificant. If only more people listened to Freeman's advice.

To imply, however, that white people are being discriminated against in this country is ludacris, and is not my argument. But in the name of diversity we are unitarily abandoning our nation's principles. The reality is that no matter how hard we try, there will always be racial imbalance and unequal representation in our schools, universities, and jobs. This is not due to racial profiling, prejudice, or lack of opportunity, yet it rather effectively corresponds with the racial makeup of a nation that is 77% White, 13% Black, and 18% Hispanic.[14] The truth is that without Affirmative Action, universities will most likely be less diversified and will most certainly hold a White/Asian American majority due to White population majority and the educational expectations of Asian cultures. What most people need to realize is that it's *ok* that this would be occurring, because in this way, everyone who gets accepted to a university or job will know that they've *earned* it independently, without government interference.

One of the major flaws of modern problem-solving techniques is always searching for complex answers to, realistically, simplistic problems, or problems that really were never problems to begin with. A 'problem' that was truly nonexistent is cultural diversity, and our answers have transformed it into a problem. In this instance, the most effective way to deal with it is to simply ignore any racial or cultural aspects of a student in terms of deciding admission, to eliminate any factors that a person has no control over in influencing the decision. It is the fairest, least biased way that encourages achievement and work-ethic once again. Affirmative Action was necessary in the 60's when it was first implemented, but our culture and racial acceptance has improved immensely since then.

Racial diversity is definitely a major component of a post-racial society; however, it should never be forced. There are ways we can increase the probability of increased diversity through more indirect means, such as creating a stabilized economy and providing streamlined access to financial assistance such as financial student aid and scholarships. If we continue down this path of disproportionate allocation of government assistance, we will never become a post-racial society. This isn't about 'black privilege' or 'minority privilege', but rather equal privilege for all without regard to race or sex. The day we stop labeling others as 'black people' or 'white people', is the day that we have become a post-racial society. The day that any kind of racial slander-not just those perpetrated towards minorities, is deemed unacceptable, is the day we have become a post-racial society. The day that we stop prioritizing one form of racism over another and start analyzing each form equally, is the day that we have become a post-racial society. Most importantly, the day that we value one another based solely on interior rather than exterior reasons is the day that we have set the universal bar in how a modern society should operate and the moral standards that one should strive for.

Imagine how frustrating it would be to be denied acceptance to a university because of your skin color. Imagine how pathetic you would feel if you were accepted only because of your skin color, not because of what you've accomplished. Why do we value others based on factors they cannot control? If we wish to apologize for how this nation treated minorities in the past, handouts and unfair boosts should never be the answer. What we do instead, is create a system that welcomes all and excludes none. We create a system that provides limitless opportunity for everyone regardless of race. We become the shining city on the hill that people worldwide strive to live, that countries worldwide strive to model. But most crucially, we don't repeat the mistakes of the past, which proves that we have truly learned from our deficiencies and are always striving to better ourselves and one another. In reference to diversity, let the cards lie where they fall, gradually yet assuredly it will develop and prosper as long as we continue to just treat one another as fellow Americans.

There will always be those who play the blame game, there will always be Jesse Jacksons and Al Sharptons, but it is imperative that their hateful rhetoric be ignored and condemned. The nation we live in now would not be one that MLK Jr. would find sufficient, not because of how minorities are treated, but rather because race is *still* a factor in judgement. It's because hate speech is allowed as long as it's directed towards a specific race (we all know which one), as if that race doesn't know what suffering is. Needless to say, history begs to differ  We have all suffered, and we all need to come together to eliminate discrimination permanently.

## Chapter 8: Corporate Giants & the One-Percent

Ever wonder where the vast majority of the world's wealth resides? If you are unsure, then you either live in the mountains or simply don't pay attention to current events. The infamous one-percent and large corporations would be the culprit here; those inconsiderate, greedy fat cats are the sole reason why we have people starving in our nation. The first-half of the previous sentence is factual, the second being a very common stereotype being used to label the wealthy. Wealth distribution is a constant hot-topic in US politics, especially with the 2016 election, where a filthy-rich businessman and wealthy Secretary of State duke it out for president. The common interpretation we receive from the media, and even other rich people, is the idea that the top one-percent and greedy corporatism is guilty for why the lower classes often struggle; basically the hoarding of wealth.

Statistically, the hoarding of wealth is most likely factual in numerous cases, but we need to realize that those who basically sit on piles of cash can and should be allowed to, and suggesting otherwise would be severe government intrusion. Others see such a philosophy differently, most notably people like Bernie Sanders, whose entire presidential campaign revolved around criticizing corporations, banks, and the one-percent. His central philosophy is, through his own words during a CNBC interview "If you have seen a massive transfer of wealth from the middle class to the top one-tenth of 1 percent, you know what, we've got to transfer that back if we're going to have a vibrant middle class", with other key areas being around the idea that the top one-percent don't "Pay their fair share" in federal income taxes.[7] The idea suggestively resonated well with millennials in particular, especially those in student loan debt or facing financial difficulties. Many are willing to believe this kind of 'miracle' cure to nationwide poverty to be the extraction of more money from the upper class.

Doing so would actually 'fix' (using the term loosely) poverty because the high upper-class collectively yields more than enough wealth to house, clothe, and nourish every impoverished person nationwide. Bernie Sanders is correct in assuming that we currently are facing a massive wealth distribution gap between the upper-class and everyone else. In 2013, the top 10% of families held 76% of the total national wealth, and the bottom half only accounted for 1%.[1] Wealth inequality is most certainly real, but by the structuring of this nation, it is not 'unfair'. Solving any form of financial burden in this country can seemingly be accomplished by withdrawing more and more from the uber-wealthy, and why not? Why not put their money to good use instead of them wasting it on another private jet? And what's the issue with it if they're just greedy hoarders to begin with? Just like with the other topics previously discussed, we do not live in a black-and-white world with concrete, definitive answers that produce no negative consequences. There will always be two sides to every circumstance.

The United States harbors one of the most extreme cases of wealth inequality due to the facts listed previously, and that eight of the ten wealthiest billionaires worldwide originate from the United States.[2] It's understandable that our situation could entice suspicion, but is wealth inequality *truly* the issue here, or is it simply an inevitable by-product of free-market Capitalism? One could argue that our higher population of millionaires and billionaires is positive, because it showcases the ability to accumulate wealth here in the US with our array of opportunities. On the other hand, is that earned wealth simply a fallacy and in reality, most of our millionaires inherited that wealth, giving a misleading notion? Surprisingly (To some), data reveals that the majority of the world's high upper-class *did* earn that wealth rather than through birth. Out of the 1826 billionaires worldwide, 1,191 were self-made and only 230 inherited their wealth, while the remaining 405 inherited some but are still building upon that wealth (Think Donald Trump and his small loan of a million dollars). Another noteworthy aspect is the growing number of female billionaires, with a 15% increase (197 vs 172 in 2014) in 2015.[2] So the idea that wealth is inherited is only 12.6 - 35% factual (35% if you include the 405 partially inherited billionaires). In other words, our staggering number of uber-wealthy individuals could easily provide evidence that our opportunities in the US do allow the growth of unimaginable riches.

This leads to another important question; with all of this money, how much do large companies and ultra-rich individuals contribute to our world, or is the money truly just being hoarded? In order to answer this, we must first investigate how much is given to charity. On one hand, a 2014 study from the Chronicle of Philanthropy revealed that Americans who earned at least $200,000 donated 5% less to charity in 2012 than in 2006.[9] Comparatively, those that are more generous donators (known as ultra-high net worth philanthropists) donate approximately 10% of their net worth. According to The Wealth-X and Arton Capital Major Giving Index, the number of UHNW's increased to 220 in 2013, the highest since

2006.[3] Overall, the rich are generally donating less, while those that do donate extensively are increasing, which generates mixed results that provide sufficient evidence to either side of the argument. Some theories suggest that the reason why the rich donate less could be due to our currently unpredictable economy, and they aren't willing to risk it. Perhaps it could be due to new evidence of charity fraud, perhaps some are just greedy. Either way, it's *their* choice.

Generally, the donations may not be extensive, but that doesn't mean the wealthy are not paying sufficient quantities to our government. In fact, the reality is far from that all-too-common preconception when evaluating tax allocation percentages. The United States may be well-known for wealth inequality, but another important aspect to consider is that, according to a 2008 study from the Organization for Economic Cooperation and Development (OECD), our nation "Has the most progressive tax system and collects the largest share of taxes from the richest 10% of the population."[6] How is this possible? The data confirms that this finding should not come as a surprise, but rather as a certainty. In 2012, the top 50 percent of all taxpayers contributed 97.2 percent of all income taxes, while the lower 50 percent paid the remaining 2.8 percent. The income gap further widens upon reaching the wealthiest one-percent; in 2013 they paid a greater share of income taxes (37.8 percent) than the bottom 90 percent combined (30.2 percent). This is because the average tax rate is approximately 8 times higher for the one-percent compared to the bottom 50 percent (27.1% versus 3.3%).[5] Unsurprisingly, these are not frequent statistics one would hear from the progressive left, as our current situation solidifies our dependency on the wealthiest to pay for our modern money-hungry government.

There is another component to be taken into account in regards to taxes. Because of the additional spending cash that the super-rich acquire, the top one-percent invests more and in greater frequency than any other socio-economic class. Investments in the stock market, as well as the purchasing/re-selling of businesses and property, is the most common source of revenue for the ultra-wealthy, therefore most, if not all sources of income will be in the form of capital gain.[10/11] The capital gain tax rate does increase for wealthier residents at 20 percent for the top 39.6% tax bracket, but overall the general tax rate for capital gains are lower than earned income tax rates.[12] This could be a benefactor for Bernie's arguments, but there are justifications for the lower capital gain tax rates. It's understandable to interpret this differential as a form of work-punishment, and an indirect supplement for the wealthy, but there are valid arguments which support the idea. The capital gain tax does not adjust for inflation; therefore, investors must pay for the inflation created by the Federal Reserve on top of the initial payment, thus cancelling out any additional rates on earned income tax rates. Additionally, lower capital gain taxes have historically assisted with an overall increase of government revenue. When President Bush enacted a cut in the top rate from 20% to 15%, revenue more than doubled from $51.3 billion in 2003 to $137.1 billion in 2007.[13] Once again, a deeper analysis provides us with new insight for the lower tax rates, so the conspiracy theories can be expelled. Capital gains can be complex to decipher, yet they are a prime example of how our government can flourish without excessive taxation.

It's virtually impossible to deny our dependency on the ultra-wealthy, given that the United States has the highest tax rates in the world for the upper class. What would be the implications of over-taxation, theoretically to the point where some of our richest would rather immigrate to another country with more lenient taxation? Under the Obama Administration, the general tax rate for the top one-percent has increased by 6 percent since he took office, which not only solidifies our lead in progressive taxation, but further entices those that which to preserve their wealth into moving their businesses elsewhere.[14] The stabilization of tax rates, therefore, should be a major priority for the Trump administration. If a significant amount of our nation's wealthiest were to leave, the US government would forfeit a large majority of tax revenue, which would financially cripple our nation and plunge us into economic despair. Lowering taxes on the one-percent is a possibility, but another solution could be (much needed) reduced government spending, or simply implementing wiser spending methods. For example, in 2010 alone the US government depleted over $223 million in multiple, arguably absurd areas which included studying male Vietnamese prostitutes, creating environmental additives on long-vacant buildings, and building an office for former Speaker of the House Dennis Hastert (Which he rarely even visits).[15] Perhaps if our government only used our tax dollars when necessary, it wouldn't require such excessive taxation to compensate for government spending.

Of course, the idea of reduced taxation for the one-percent is commonly affiliated with conservative ideals, so would the stereotype of rich allegiance with the Republican Party be accurate? Do Democrats hold validity in claiming to be the party of the working-class while the GOP's alliance is with the ultra-wealthy? The data concludes that in terms of party support, the idea is simply a common stereotype. Up until the 1980's, the Republican Party held the lead in ultra-wealthy support in terms of financial contributions for campaigns, but the lead has gradually shifted since then; from 1982 to 2012, the Republican share of contributions has declined from 68% to 59% from the *Forbes 400* (List of the 400 wealthiest individuals in America). In contrast, the Democratic Party has been experiencing a surge in super-rich donations; between 1980 and 2012, the share of campaign contributions from the top .01 percent of adults has increased from 7% to 25%.[8] Within a few years, the overall support from the ultra-wealthy will equalize, and if the current shift continues, it won't be long before the Democratic Party will be dubbed the party of the rich. The culprit is most likely the result of a growing number of elite millennials, who in general are more supportive of the Democratic Party. Nonetheless, the debunking of wealthy affiliation towards one specific party remains valid. The general mindset of the one-percent is becoming more diverse, much like the general culture of our nation.

The national discussion over wealth inequality will always be a controversial topic here in the states, because on one hand, it's not difficult to view our ever-widening wealth inequality as a negative reflection on American corporatism and an emphasis on materialistic greed. But what must be taken into consideration is how unequal our taxation system is in comparison, because while wealth accumulation is primarily under the control of the individual, how our taxes are spent and the amounts extracted from our income is set by the government. The beauty of the United States is the ability for one to climb the economic ladder either through hard work, investing, entrepreneurship, or maybe by winning the lottery. Contrary to popular belief, the ultra-rich are not responsible for the poverty of a nation, in fact, due to the excessive taxes they must pay, the ultra-rich are indirectly improving the opportunities in this nation. But of course, it's the government's responsibility to properly utilize the taxes to assist those in need. In short, the wealthy supply the income (As with the rest of us), but the federal and state governments must effectively allocate the revenue in areas that *really* matter, not spending $3 million in studying World of Warcraft.[15]

None of this, however, implies that the wealthy are more important than the rest of us; the entire purpose of the initial argument is to simply reinforce the notion that the wealthy *do* pay their fair share in taxes, and the idea that perhaps our government relies *too* much on taxing the wealthy to provide the majority of our federal revenue. Yet despite what the wealthy (most commonly through mandates) gives to the nation, I am still a firm believer that the middle working-class is the backbone of our nation. In general, we all play our own specific role in the continuation of our country, because we need the investors of the upper class, the job-suppliers of corporations and small businesses, and the employees that create the goods, run the facilities, defend our borders, teach our children, and carry out the daily jobs that maintain the turning of the wheel. We are not defined by our materialistic wealth, and nobody ought to acquire a superiority complex for being wealthier than another. But it's ridiculous to accuse the wealth of another for one's own financial struggles, for such an excuse is invalid in a nation where the majority of its richest individuals *earned* their wealth, most commonly from the ground up. While there are exceptions, the most common culprit for one's financial burdens is oneself and nobody else. Jealousy is an all-too-frequent trait in modern society, so I can guarantee that the rich man across the street doesn't have a damn thing to do with why you're incapable of purchasing the new iPhone 7. If anyone is to blame for the difficulty of finding employment, or struggling to pay for college, it'd be the rules and regulation enforced by either the local, state, or federal government. Otherwise, we are all responsible for our own success.

## *Chapter 9*: **Educational Collapse**

In the modern era, receiving a proper education is nearly a mandate in order to thrive as a successful citizen. School is the first real avenue where students, who up until now, have only been exposed to the beliefs and values of their family, and are now thrust into an environment of new exposure to differing opinions. The revelation of new opinions will result in one of two aftermaths; it will either strengthen the opinions one already holds, or it will sway one's opinions in a new direction. Either way, it will assist in the formation of a well-rounded citizen that understands both sides of an argument, and therefore can formulate educated opinions. Receiving an education provides students with a basic overview of life's components, in an objective method that allows students to process the information as they see fit.

But this flood of information is essentially useless if students forget it after each test, but what schools instill is in the form of exercising the brain to be able to solve problems and to think critically, which is an obvious requirement to survive in society. So while there may be a minutely minimal chance of using the derivative of a tangent slope in the real world, it *does* teach us how to process and perceive complex problems. A basic rule that schools adhere to is '*How* to think, not *what* to think.' A historical representation of when the education system reversed that idea would be along the lines of *Hitler's Youth* during the 1930's and 40's, where teenage boys were indoctrinated to follow the Nazi agenda. A proper education does not brainwash its subjects; instead it provides information from *both* points of view, for revealing just one side *is* indoctrination, because differing opinions are never revealed.

Just like how the school system was manipulated during World War 2, public education is a sensitive and easily exploitable system that can indoctrinate an entire civilization if under complete control. Psychology tells us that the younger people are taught a certain way, the more likely they will continue following that line of belief through their adult lives. So if the school system begins indoctrination when kids are as young as preschoolers and kindergarteners, the risks of deviation will plummet and the hordes of sheep will continue to expand. This is how the Nazi party effectively raised their *Hitler Youth* program to 2.3 million members by 1933.[1] Another interesting fictional demonstration of nationalized indoctrination (that's begun to form startling similarities with today's society) is the novel *1984* by George Orwell. If history has taught us one thing, it's that our education should never be used for means of control, because complete control is virtually unstoppable if accessed.

In chapter four I discussed how colleges are using subtle forms of indoctrination on their students, but the effects of doing so with higher education is not as detrimental as when students are exposed to indoctrination over the course of their entire education. Fortunately enough, students are generally firm in their beliefs by the time they attend a university, but the brain is a sponge during childhood. I do not, however, believe that public education is attempting to brainwash America's youth, but our current education system *is* deviating from its original purposes. I was not specifically referencing the schools of our nation during the first two paragraphs;

I was outlining how education *should* operate, and why it was created initially. Recently, our education system has begun to deteriorate in several key areas.

As incredible as the United States is, the one area where our weakness is apparent is in education. The US is ranked 14th out of 40 listed nations in education, which specifies as 'Cognitive skills and educational attainment', and ranked 17th in educational performance by the Economist Intelligence Unit. According to the Program for International Student Assessment, the US is ranked 24th in literacy.[2] Logical reasoning would imply that due to the strong economy and fluid opportunities that this nation provides, our scores should be significantly higher. (I am aware that unlike many other countries, we test students of varying abilities, but studies have shown that our best-performing students our out-performed by students in European countries.[4]) Clearly this indicates room for improvement in those areas, so who or what is the culprit? Every major dilemma that our education system experiences can all be categorized into one simple aspect: Lack of Innovation and/or listening to the needs of local communities, with the first and foremost problem being a lack of public K-12 funding. In 2015, the Center on Budget and Policy Priorities discovered that 34 states have decreased funding on a per student basis than they did before the recession, and states are responsible for 44% of the total education budget.[3] If anything, investing more into education would generate substantial returns since an educated population generates more wealth, therefore contributing more into the economy.

In regards to a lack of innovation, as of current our education system has remained unchanged in terms of accommodating students with differing talents and strengths. In an actual literal sense, our system lumps every student together and expects the same result regardless of the student's abilities. For being the most diverse nation on the planet, that kind of system is a failure from the beginning and the statistics prove it. The problem has been a continual nuisance even a century ago, with a satirical piece created by an Illinois newspaper in 1903 called the "Jungle School Board", which identified the differences among students in the form of animals. An alteration was made and published by the *Boston Herald* in 1946 which specifically alludes to how the education system attempts to create average students by not allowing them to focus on their talents. The excerpt follows:

*One time the animals had a school. The curriculum consisted of running, climbing, flying, and swimming, and all the animals took all of the subjects.*

*The Duck was good in swimming—better, in fact, than his instructor—and he made passing grades in flying, but he was practically hopeless in running. Because he was low in this subject, he was made to stay after school and drop his swimming class in order to practice running. He kept this up until he was only average in swimming, but average was passing so nobody worried about that except the duck.*

*The Eagle was considered a problem pupil and was disciplined severely. He beat all the others to the top of the tree in the climbing class, but he always used his own way of getting there.*

*The Rabbit started at the top of the class in running, but he had a nervous breakdown and had to drop out of school on account of so much make-up work in swimming.*

*The Squirrel led the climbing class, but his flying teacher made him start his flying from the ground up instead of from the top down, and he developed charley horses from overexertion at the takeoff and began getting C's in climbing and D's in running.*

*The practical Prairie Dogs apprenticed their offspring to the Badgers when the school authorities refused to add digging to the curriculum.*

*At the end of the year, an abnormal Eel that could swim well and run, climb, and fly a little was made Valedictorian.*[6]

Perhaps just a cute little fable, but its validity held 70 years ago, and is still valid today. Our current system fails to recognize the talents of each student, and instinctively assumes that everyone can be a good test-taker instead. The truth is that some students are stronger with hands-on activities; others are more skilled with tests. Some perform better with tests when listening to music or chewing gum, with others it's not needed. None of these differentials matter to the curriculum set by Common Core, which even fails to take into account the differences among communities and states, which prior to the installation of Common Core have been able to instruct their students with agendas that have been localized to meet the demands of their respective communities. Basically, when students with varying abilities are cast into the same system for the same period of time, while being expected to understand the same material, inevitably the curriculum's difficulty will have to decrease to meet those expectations. This in turn produces an overall mediocre education which results in our nation's low rankings in educational assessments.

A method that some other countries use, particularly the ones that have scored exceptionally well on the PISA (Program for International Student Assessment) exam, such as China, Finland, and Switzerland, have developed separate tracks for students who are entering high school. Students can either engage with the traditional academic track, which is the standard academic process of in-class work and testing, or there is the vocational track which circulates around more hands-on and visual work.[4] This way, students are given the choice to attend whichever program best accommodates their needs, which also allows for more rigorous courses since most of the students attending are more prepared, skilled, and knowledgeable. If the United States would simply expand the opportunities for vocational academics, the average intellect (as well as enjoyment) of the student body would improve considerably. It is nothing more than the recognition that every person is different. Instead of the duck being graded on its ability to run, it would only be assessed on its original strengths-swimming and flying, just like the squirrel would be graded on its climbing skills, and the rabbit on its running ability. A student's potential can only be released if encouraged.

The ridiculous quantity of tests that students have to endure in this country also releases educational stagnation. In 2015, a study from a new council of the Great City Schools discovered that a typical student takes 112 mandated standardized tests from preschool through 12th grade, whereas most nations that score higher than the United States on international exams test their students, on average, only 3 times during their school careers.[5] The emphasis on performing well on these tests also burdens the students and causes monumental amounts of stress. With our education system, a single poor performance on a standardized test (Think ACT/SAT) can prevent a student from attending the university of his/her dreams. We place such a massive pedestal under test-taking that our education system fails to recognize that not everyone is skilled in such areas, and their opportunities are severely restricted when tests dictate such a huge portion of their lives.

Testing has recently stemmed beyond just affecting the students; teachers themselves now must rely on appropriate test scores from the students because they are now used to evaluate their performance, essentially mandating teachers to only instruct material that will best allow students to score adequately, basically 'Teaching to the test', which hinders methods such as teaching with an individualized curriculum. The policy of No Child Left Behind has accelerated this process, and in many cases to the point where lunch and recess must be cut to accommodate.[7] Students and teachers both are cast under intense pressure to perform adequately on tests, because failing to do so could result in a student not being able to attend a university or even graduate, whereas a teacher could either be fired or receive lower paychecks if his/her students fail to perform to state standards.

The infamous program known as Common Core has sparked heated controversy since its creation in 2009. Stereotypically it has been known, particularly due to President Obama's extended praise of it, as a federal mandate among the states. While it may not be mandatory, it *was* essentially used as a bribe-reason being why 45 states almost immediately signed up after its implementation.[10] Any state that implements Common Core will receive higher incentives for federal grant funds, and given the increasingly scarce resources among schools (especially in my community), many states didn't have much of a choice.[8] The issue with this initial lure is that the cost of actually using Common Core is phenomenally severe; the total net cost of the program in my home state of Michigan costed taxpayers $569 million, while the national total for 7 years of the Common Core Standards Initiative (CCSI) was $15.8 billion.[9] Common Core originally emphasized good intentions, and during its creation, it appeared to be the final solution in solving America's educational crisis by encouraging critical thinking rather than the typical memorization followed by regurgitation process.

This leads to the question: Has Common Core actually been successful in its prospects? The short answer is 'No' because of the ways that Common Core actually evaluates student intellect, by using the ancient (outdated) method of testing. Common Core uses testing as a base-line in evaluating academic progress, which is problematic because, according to a 2012 Washington Post article by Veteran teacher Marion Brady "The Common Core Standards are a set-up for national standardized tests, tests that can't evaluate complex thought, can't avoid cultural bias, can't measure non-verbal learning, can't predict anything of consequence".[10] This basically states that the tests given out by Common Core, while they argue are different than other tests, truthfully resemble little difference. Just like any other test, these assessments cannot take environmental, genetic, or circumstantial factors into consideration, all of which affect test scores.

American values of individualism and nonconformity are also getting the boot with Common Core. The idea of meeting a 'standard' most nearly means 'conformity' in every sense of the word, and the only component truly being standardized are the minds of the students, particularly with the more vulnerable, sponge-like minds of younger students. The entire idea of establishing critical thought could be considered counterintuitive, because students are so hardwired to memorize for testing that the process almost imitates the memorization/regurgitation method. Since the tests also use multiple-choice questions, this disallows students the ability to think deeply about certain topics with the lack of short essays, which are instead often used with Advanced Placement exams.

According to Michael Benezra, a legislative director for the Massachusetts Senate (The state that has also been considered the 'success story' of Common Core), students often forget the 'big picture' on major topics because "The reliance on testing pigeonholes the teachers to teach only to the test... So the kids are coming out and what they're learning might not be conventional. So they might know some obscure facts about American history, but they might miss why the revolution started."[8] The importance of being able to comprehend the overall concept from certain topics assists in developing a well-rounded citizen. In the real-world, knowing minute increments of details does little good, since they virtually cannot be applied. Utilizing concepts, themes, and overall messages can be used to guide the decision-making process of any person. Common Core may very well be producing opposite effects from the original schemas, because students are so focused on simply performing adequately on tests that the entire concept of receiving an education is manipulated. Testing in itself is beneficial because it allows teachers to evaluate the progress of their students, but an overexertion of testing can turn severe and highly stressful, and when it's the only aspect being considered in evaluating academic achievement, that's when you reveal a failing, outdated education system.

The testing is reinforced through an increase in academic complexity and difficulty which Common Core presents. This is fine for students such as myself, but for a good majority of students, the higher rigorous schedule causes even larger amounts of stress. This could be partly the culprit for our international rankings; students are obtaining an education that few are actually prepared for, and they suffer even more greatly on tests as a result. One such example of how academic performance has been jeopardized from Common Core can be located in the schools of New York City. After Common Core was introduced in 2012, in 2013 the overall passing percentage of students in lower-performing schools plummeted by 66 percent, and in higher-performing schools it fell by 16 percent.[13] Therefore, students who struggle more have suffered more, which has also indirectly affected impoverished families the greatest. The increased difficulty is good theoretically, but without proper guidance, the idea backfires almost immediately.

So how do we 'fix' our current system? Most economic dilemmas can be solved with a greater allocation of funding, which would assist in reducing shutdown frequencies of schools (Several have closed in my community over the past few years), which would in turn help alleviate the increasing, and therefore less personalized classroom populations which have had to accommodate for the students immigrating from closed schools. This would also of course introduce up-to-date technology and textbooks to enhance the educational experience, and could be used to hire additional counselors, educational psychologists, and therapists to assist struggling students, which would help in performing more efficiently with the increased academic rigorousness. Another primary factor that deserves reexamination is the emphasis on testing, which has grown considerably more severe under No Child Left Behind and Common Core. Reducing the quantity of tests, along with the length of tests that are especially prevalent with the ACT/SAT (3.58/3.8 hours), which can cause a gradual deterioration in performance through fatigue.[11/12] Common Core should also face re-evaluation; every state should at least investigate the impact of Common Core in their area, and assess whether or not keeping the program would be beneficial. And lastly, we must be willing to acknowledge and help develop the specified talents and abilities of each student, by offering multiple pathways that best suits their needs. This will enable students to achieve greater success and fulfillment in their careers.

Our nation is in tremendous debt, this is obvious, along with the fact that we truthfully have little funds to share. What must be acknowledged, however, is the impact that additional funding would have on our education. The returns would far surpass the initial investment, for an educated society generates far more wealth than an uneducated one, which would help stimulate the economy.

Receiving a proper, worthwhile education is crucial in maintaining success, not just financially, but success in life. People often say 'Ignorance is bliss'-that people are simply content with not being knowledgeable and are happy because of it. I disagree. The only way one can truly impact and better the world is through knowledge and understanding, which begins with receiving an education. Education can be simplified as being the foundation of our future; inventors, engineers, entrepreneurs, and the great scientists of history did not acquire their knowledge through imagination, but through the acquiring of knowledge by being educated. Modern society would disintegrate without it, so we must proceed in every necessary step into ensuring that the students of today receive the best possible education they can.

## Chapter 10: International Deterioration

7:00 am. The year was 1941. The morning scent was obscurely calm, with the usual frost blanketing the naval machinery that encompassed the harbor like an impenetrable fortress. Christmas was fast-approaching, yet the realization never dawned upon the American sailors who continued training, watching, and anticipating the ambiguous situation that they reside in. The US heartland was a couple thousand miles East, yet the concept of fragile exposure never infiltrated the thoughts of the soldiers, who scoffed at the possibility that the new, advanced equipment of the US Navy could be penetrated. Pearl Harbor was a castle in a wasteland, with dozens of ships scattering the bay like knights protecting their king. The war had been progressing for several years now, yet to the Americans, the conflict appeared to be located half a world away, which caused some to question the importance of just waiting and anticipating.

7:30 am. Every individual already awake and alert, with the routine activities commencing at full pace. Nothing appeared unordinary; nothing seemed out-of-place except the serene calmness that enveloped the bay.

7:50 am. A low, distant rumbling materialized in the distance. Such a noise had been heard before, which produced little concern among the populace. The communal activities resumed as scheduled.

7:55 am. The alarms have been struck. An army, seemingly created out of the clouds themselves due to its unanticipated appearance, began launching a full-frontal assault against the unprepared Naval fleet. 200 Japanese aircraft descended upon the Americans, dropping explosives that disintegrated any unfortunate being that lay in its path. Sailors witnessed the horror of that impenetrable defense being helplessly obliterated, along with fellow soldiers that they called 'companion' and 'friend' being slaughtered like cattle. Help was unavailable, relief was nonexistent, death was inevitable.

In total, 2,400 US personnel were killed, and 18 ships were destroyed. Such an unprecedented attack marked the greatest retaliatory response in US history. Previously, the nation was split between the anti-war 'Isolationists' and the pro-war 'Hawks', who have now rallied together to join the war effort with overwhelming support in the US Senate (82-0) and the House (388-1).[19] With the US now leading the Alliance, the war abruptly ceased with the nuclear destruction of Nagasaki on August 9, 1945, which forced a permanent surrender by the Japanese government.[20] First initiating during World War 1 and continuing during World War 2, the United States implanted its position as the prominent world superpower.

After the use of the two nuclear bombs, the United States was undoubtedly feared and respected for its military prowess, and the attack on Pearl Harbor, while detrimental, was also the primary indication that, according to Japanese Admiral Isoroku Yamamoto, "I fear all we have done is to awaken a sleeping giant and fill him with a terrible resolve."[21] This was stated after the Pearl Harbor assault. The United States was the most feared and respect nation on the planet after essentially rescuing the Allied forces and assisting with the annihilation of the Axis powers. Since then, we would become the dominant leader of NATO and (would be) the dominant power in the League of Nations if we accepted the invitation. This time period solidified both our dominance on the battlefield and as a force for positive change; permanently transforming our prior isolationist position.

But much like a football player expected to maintain his starting position and continually proving his worth, or else discarded for a more qualified player, the US is also expected to maintain its position as a leader, or else replaced with another. Since the Cold War, the prominent threat to global peace has not been a solitary nation, but rather the spread of terrorism. This threat is difficult to assess, as the spheres of influence by terrorist organizations are scattered, along with revenue deposits and even the terrorists themselves; they often mask themselves among civilian populations and wear civilian clothing. Nonetheless, it is still a threat that the US is expected to control with our state-of-the-art technological capabilities and overwhelming military strength. The modern tragic irony is our current incapability in suppressing terrorism, yet we managed to defeat the Nazis and the Japanese. As a nation, we are gradually becoming less feared, less respected, and increasingly becoming more lenient in our retaliations.

The foreign policies being implemented over the past eight years has accumulated dire consequences, the most obvious one being the rise and spread of ISIS. The origins of the Islamic State of Iraq and Syria supposedly derived as an extension of Al-Qaeda, yet ISIS now has replaced Al-Qaeda as the dominant terrorist organization. Tom Sanderson, a terrorism expert at the Center for Strategic and International Studies, once told CBS News that "(ISIS) is more significant and more varied than what al Qaeda had in terms of its actual combat capabilities where they are fielding artillery. They are holding much greater territory than al Qaeda had, they are governing people, they have a more diverse funding base... they have a greater localized funding base than al Qaeda." Sanderson also argued that "(Al-Qaeda) simply did not have the technology that ISIS has now; the social networking that enables them to reach a much greater audience." With the addition of social networking, advantages which were simply unavailable to Al-Qaeda during its time, has allowed ISIS to rapidly multiply in strength. An estimated 10-20,000 foreigners have joined the ranks of ISIS thus far, including 100-200 Americans, along with the increasing threat of homegrown 'Lone Wolf' terrorists.

According to some, the mounting strength of ISIS is not completely the result of the Obama Administration, yet instead originated from the Clinton Administration extending through the Bush Administration. According to Juan Zarate, CBS News' Senior National Security Analyst, the US has failed to suppress ISIS because "...We had certainly not done enough through the '90s and into 2001 to disrupt al Qaeda's infrastructure, training, plotting and in some ways we've allowed ISIS to gain a foothold by being fairly inactive in Syria to date..." This indicates a lack of prioritization from the last three presidents in terms of sufficiently and effectively eliminating the growth of ISIS.[17] The sustained and largely uninterrupted expansion of ISIS can be verified through the numbers: In 2016, CIA Director John Brennan reported ISIS population details to the US Senate, which included 18-22,000 in Syria and Iraq; 5-8,000 in Libya; approximately 7,000 spread out in Syria, Libya, and Nigeria, and several hundred each in Egypt,

Yemen, Afghanistan, and Pakistan.[18] With such alarming numbers, the possibility of committing terrorism is also approaching unprecedented rates; in 2015 alone, 11,774 terrorist attacks occurred across 92 countries which resulted in 28,300 deaths. While the attacks have decreased by 13% compared to 2014, the decline was only the first time since 2012.[8]

Then-President Obama's primary retaliatory method was the use of airstrikes. The idea was to prevent the possibility of US military personnel being harmed, but the method was simply insufficient in halting terrorist progress. In a 2015 report, ISIS managed to double its territorial control despite the approximately 800 coalition airstrikes used against them; a third of Syria fell under their influence as a result.[5] Yet despite the assumption that ISIS is now more globally dangerous than the caliphate responsible for committing the most horrific terrorist attack on US soil in history, our underestimation of the strength of ISIS was arguably a root cause for their success. Most remember Obama's comment on ISIS: "If a JV team puts on Lakers uniforms, that doesn't make them Kobe Bryant." Currently, the President leaves office with 5,262 U.S. troops still in Iraq, 8,400 in Afghanistan, and 503 in Syria, with a total of over 8,000 airstrikes from more than 13 countries that still fails to suppress a caliphate 35,000 strong.[6/7]

Despite its numerous attacks and increasing prowess, ISIS is not the most fearsome consequence from ineffective foreign policies; several national relations are on the brink of collapse, which may very well possibly result in war. One such nation which has been circulating in the media is Russia, when the spotlight first dawned upon them during the Ukraine invasion, and even more intensely after the Democratic National Convention and Presidential election hacking accusations. The Ukraine conflict was the center for national attention during 2014-2015; Russia annexed Ukraine's southern Crimea peninsula in 2014 by force, which many argue violated the United Nations General Assembly Resolution 2625 (XXV) which states 'The territory of a State shall not be the object of acquisition by another State resulting from the threat or use of force'.[2] The apparent violation sparked minimal retaliation from the UN, largely because of the vast Russian nuclear arsenal that many fear would cause nuclear fallout. Some sanctions were the only consequence that the Russian Federation experienced, and it's rather unsurprising that such a response would invoke little change from Vladimir Putin's plans.

A total of over 9,700 deaths have resulted from the conflict, with an eventual ceasefire which was implemented in February of 2015 that has experienced frequent violations.[1] In recent years, this crisis was among the first signals of a deteriorating relationship between the United States and Russia. Afterwards, other worrisome incidents propelled this assumption. Such events include an American spy working undercover in Moscow who is tackled and beaten at the gates of a U.S. Embassy, and a Russian fighter jet flying within 30 feet of a U.S. Naval ship. Brian Katulis, a senior fellow at the Center for American Progress, claims that "...this is probably the lowest point we've seen in U.S.-Russian relations since the Soviet invasion of Afghanistan in 1979."[13] The statement's validity has recently only been made more apparent when the FBI and CIA have both concluded the Russian interference of the 2016 US election as being factual in December of 2016.[11] The State

Department responded by extraditing 35 Russian intelligence operatives in the U.S. and shutting down two Russian compounds in Maryland and New York. The Russian Embassy in the UK then responded by tweeting a picture of a lame duck while identifying it as "Cold War Deja Vu", along with Vladimir Putin's spokesperson announcing the consideration of a retaliation.[10]

Unless immediate action is implemented to reverse our current relations with Russia; the consequences will be detrimental if a possible military conflict initiates between the two superpowers. The nuclear warheads controlled by the United States and Russia alone comprise as being more than 90% of the total global arsenal, with the US owning 6,800 and Russia owning 7000 according to an update in January of 2017.[3] While the United States does contain the most advanced missile defense system in the world; no modern system could possibly deflect the possibility of up to a thousand ICBMs being launched simultaneously, all hurtling towards our largest, most populous urban districts. Unquestionably, waging war against Russia would result in catastrophic amounts of casualties on both sides, despite our larger, more advanced military. World War 3 would quickly erupt; the allies of both nations joining the conflict. Of course, such a possibility is small, but if our relations with Russia continue to deteriorate, then the risks of such a possibility will only increase.

Relations have also begun to crumble with our strongest allies, not just our known adversaries. The United States and Israel share many similarities in terms of economies, government operations, and military prowess. Combine that with our continual financial and military support such as the creation of the Iron Dome;

our relationship with Israel has remained strong. Considered the 'America in the Middle East', Israel has historically been widely known as a safe-haven for migrants from the surrounding nations that are well-known for violating human rights, such as Saudi Arabia, Pakistan, and Syria. Israel also holds vital importance to the world's three most prominent religions-Christianity, Islam, and Judaism; it is considered the Holy Land by all three, with particular attention focused on Jerusalem. With some of the most secure airports and facilities on earth; travelers are well-assured of their safety when either residing in or visiting the most developed country in the Middle-Eastern region.

But Israel is in a state of unrest. According to the results from the latest United Nations Security Council vote, 20 anti-Israel resolutions were passed in 2016, with only four for the rest of the world-one for North Korea, Syria, Iran, and Russia. Some of the accusations were borderline preposterous; the World Health Organization condemned Israel as being the only violator of "mental, physical and environmental health"; UN Women condemned the nation as being the only violator of women's rights (with no regard to the frequent misogynistic practices of nations like Afghanistan and Iran), and the International Labor Organization condemned Israel as the only violator of labor rights. But how does this tie with the specific relationship between the United States and Israel? Because Israel's strongest ally failed to defend them during the Council meeting, along with other suspicions that the United States was actually partly involved with the resolutions, largely due to our allowing of the Security Council to condemn Israeli settlements in the West Bank and east Jerusalem as a "Flagrant violation" of international law.[12]

After the election of President Donald Trump, the relationship between the United States and Israel appears to be in the process of healing, given the more friendly cooperation between Netanyahu and Trump. However, it is imperative that our nation continues to support Israel, especially as the rest of the United Nations remains adamant in their indifference towards Israel. Given the prominent position of the States in terms of UN diplomatic decisions; the responsibility of properly evaluating the decisions of Israel must be argued for future Security Council votes. This does not indicate the possibility of essentially giving the nation a free pass on any illegal acts, but we should work towards the goal that Israel is *properly* evaluated for their decisions, rather than allowing the obvious personal bias towards the country by numerous members of the United Nations to alter the votes.

Destabilization is still continuing in other nations as well. The war on Syria has unquestionably thrust the nation into chaos, with several indications of our previous administrations' weakness in controlling the situation. In August of 2012, Obama publicly warned that President Bashar Assad would cross a "Red line" if he used chemical weapons against the opposing rebellion. Unsurprisingly, Bashar ignored the threat, and slaughtered hundreds of people with poison gas in rebel-controlled parts of Damascus. And how does the former-president retaliate after the Syrian government blatantly crossed the supposed-red line? Initially, the threat appeared to be following through, with missiles, bombers, and warships prepared and ready for action. Even then-Secretary of State John Kerry gave a speech on August 30, in which he stated that an attack on Assad was imminent. But no missiles were launched, no warships deployed, and no bombers bombing military compounds. What occurred instead, was a United Nations Security Council resolution which mandated that Syria retire 1,300 tons of chemicals and other material used to make sarin nerve gas, mustard blister agent, and the production equipment; all to be discarded at sea.

James Stavridis, a retired US Navy admiral who served as NATO supreme commander until 2013, stated after the incident that "(Obama) will be judged harshly for …failing to enforce the so-called red line in Syria against Assad's use of chemical weapons."[7] While many argue that Obama's decision created a more positive aftermath-preventing a possible war and saving American lives; the issue does not dwell among the retaliation itself. The controversy erupted out of the President's failure to reinforce his threat, as it signals signs of our inability to follow through with our promises. If Obama had never warned Assad about crossing the red line, then the criticisms would not be as significant. But because he initiated an alternative response which contradicted the original warning, nations worldwide began to question our legitimacy; terrorist organizations, corrupt governments, and general enemies of the United States began assuming that we are inherently weak, which helped fuel the continuation of their illegal acts. In 1941, we completely followed through with our retaliation against the Japanese bombings on Pearl Harbor. Today, we're too scared to follow through on similar promises.

In Afghanistan, the US military and CIA have 'Turned a blind eye' as an Afghanistan government agency spends foreign donor funds on militia groups who are known for committing numerous atrocities involving human right's violations, according to local and western officials. For instance, Perim Qul, a militia leader armed by the Afghan National Directorate of Security, allegedly conducts such kinds of acts. He received $85,000 to arm 500 of his men to fight against the Taliban, yet reports arose which suggests that he spends part of those funds on a private prison where he tortures and extorts local residents, including a situation where his men have even ambushed and killed a local politician. In one interview, Perim even admits that the Taliban are not his primary enemy, but rather the local governing political party. The Afghan National Directorate of Security reportedly receives the bulk of its funding from the CIA.[16]

Six years preceding the overthrowing of Libyan dictator Moammar Gadhafi, Libya continues remaining in political, economic, and societal disaster.[9] Violating UN resolution 2231-preventing the country from conducting missile tests for eight years; Iran has already launched two ballistic missiles since the enforcement of the resolution.[14]

In 2014, the Obama Administration sidestepped a mandated 30-day congressional notification period, and accepted a prisoner exchange which involved the transferring of five Taliban war criminals for U.S. Army Sgt. Bowe Bergdahl-who was charged with desertion, one of the most reprehensible military crimes one can commit.[15] At this point, the events of Benghazi should be familiar to most of us.

But the entirety is not completely negative. After the implementation of the Iran Nuclear Deal, Iran forfeited 98 percent of its nuclear material, the number of US soldiers residing in areas of conflict have been reduced from 150,000 to 14,000, and the number of US casualties is in decline.[4/7]

Extending beyond, however, we witness a plethora of instability, unrest, and in many instances pure chaos that is enveloping multiple areas of the globe. Despite this, Obama still managed to win the Nobel Peace prize during the beginning of his administration. With the beginning of a new administration, we have an opportunity to restore our position as a leader on the global stage, but it is not guaranteed by any means. Restoring relations with Russia, maintaining our alliances with nations like Israel, and fully utilizing our military might to crush terrorist organizations such as ISIS and keeping power-hungry states like North Korea in check (which certainly includes the aspect of following through on our threats) should all be considered and prioritized. Our international policies are in disarray, and it may require years to follow to alleviate the unrest. As a nation, we were once respected by our allies and feared by our enemies, yet that position has slowly but assuredly deteriorated over the past few decades. The star quarterback isn't playing up to standard, and the competition is growing more fiercely. In order to restore our leadership position, any force that threatens the sanctity and security of world peace should be eliminated in an effective manner. Because if not, the threat may one day appear on our doorstep, as it has in the past.

## *Chapter 11*: **The Abandonment of Morality**

November 4, 2016, Friday night. The stage was dark. A tantalizing, monstrous US flag illuminated in the background, protruding an assortment of spectacles and light. The audience, not even slightly dampened by the oncoming night, continued cheering and screaming as if this night would be their last. Beams of neon-blue washed over the excited crowd, with a snake-like laser periodically encircling the white and black flag. The flag suddenly vanishes; the overhead switches to the figure of a person, holding a microphone. The roaring of the mob increases ever so drastically, and rightfully so. Reflected on the giant screen, the profile of one of the most famous rappers in modern history becomes apparent. The song hastily begins.

"Fuck with me, you know I got it. Fuck with me, you know I got it. Sexy bitch I hope she 'bout it. Come fuck with me, you know I got it." The lyrics ranged out, and still continuing with "I just landed in Europe, nigga. Shopping bags, I'm a tourist, nigga. Money talk I speak fluent, nigga. Reeboks on, I just do it, nigga..." The audience laps up the language like a dog with water, dripping from the tongue, thirsty for more. "I'm riding big coming down that beach. Geechy niggas with satin sheets. Bad bitch, she a masterpiece. Got a bad bitch, she a masterpiece." As Jay Z dominates the stage, presidential candidate Hillary Clinton tentatively and quietly waits off-stage, contemplating if her strategy in attracting young, black voters was successful.[1]

The morals of an individual, in many ways, define who they are. It is the unconscious force that guides our behavior; it dictates our ethical conduct and defines what behavior is acceptable and unacceptable. The distinction between right and wrong is unique for every individual, and the cultural standards of a nation help influence and shape our morality. Because of this, it is essential that a culture at least pays attention to the ethical values that it either reinforces or discourages, because it plays a major role in shaping the personalities of the people who dwell in it. The culture of the United States is no exception. The material that our citizens are exposed to: Television, radio, music, and recently yet perhaps the most influential being Social Media, all bombard and infiltrate the thought processes of everyone. Arguably, the morals instilled from family and relatives is most influential in shaping a person's beliefs, but the material which surrounds us on a daily occurrence can be difficult to ignore, even by the most hardened of individuals.

Considering our progress as a nation in terms of increasing our tolerance levels, to females, homosexuals, and people of ethnic minorities, it would not be difficult to argue that our moral standards have increased as a nation. If that's the case, then why do we so often hear many Baby-Boomers and the people of Generation X (Sometimes Millennials) criticizing modern moral standards? Is it due to their intolerance of other people? Rarely is that the underlying motive in the modern world, yet in many areas, their criticisms are valid. While we may have experienced drastic progression in some areas, we have also regressed in others. As a nation, it is crucial that we attempt progression in all key areas, and to disallow the values and morals that have constructed the foundation of the United States to whither in the process.

For instance, when a presidential candidate allows a rapper to spew provocative language at a concert in a desperate attempt to generate more votes, it channels the idea that such behavior is acceptable for the millions that have looked up to that person for inspiration. Or when child-hood icons like Miley Cyrus begin grinding on other men on stage; sure she retains the freedom and has every right to behave in such a way, but the repercussions for such actions can be detrimental when so many children adored her as a Disney character. Famous people play a major role in constructing the cultural identity of an entire nation, given their status and position of influential power. When the cameras are thrust upon them, social media outlets buzzing and hovering over them, their albums being advertised on iTunes, Pandora, and Spotify, and the entirety of the media covering their every move, every word which escapes from their lips, treating them almost as a deity. When celebrities are placed upon such a high pedestal, the sponge-like minds of the people who adore them will be filled with their influence.

Music is also highly influential in constructing national morals. According to a 2014 survey by Edison Research, the average US citizen listens to approximately four hours of audio per day, so our exposure to music has increased to an all-time high.[2] Because of this, the statements, themes, and values being expressed by today's popular music provides an effective outlet in tempting our beliefs and behavior. To this day, whether music influences culture, or culture influences music is up to interpretation, but regardless of which side is more valid, the one outcome will always remain the same: We as individuals are influenced by the messages being perpetrated by music. This can either be beneficial or dangerous, depending on the substance of the music, so how often are people exposed to explicit content? Audio data is scarce to locate in recent years; however, the latest extensive report from 2008 still provides insight on modern trends. The report derives from the Archives of Pediatrics and Adolescent Medicine, which discovered that one in three popular songs contains references to drug or alcohol consumption.[3] Given the increasing quantity of teens who listen to music, the opportunities for exposure of these elements are reaching unprecedented levels.

This, however, by no means suggests that music should be more regulated. The content in which artists wish to distribute is completely their decision, and they should have the freedom to do so. But it is noteworthy to highlight some of the influences of music; as such an influence is relatively new in the modern era with the increasing opportunities of obtaining music with the development of new technology. The overall standards being displayed by modern music does reflect the general moral standards of a nation in one way or another. But music artists and celebrities themselves are not to blame for such cultural shifts. The attention they receive, the popularity of their content, and the importance of their language that the media and society values plays a far greater role. A person can announce the most heinous of opinions, but if they receive the attention about the subject that they desire, then it does nothing but fuel their courage and allows them to continue.

The most important cause for the apparent decay of national morality derives from society itself; the values it emphasizes, the tolerance of certain activities, and its willingness in accepting dissenting viewpoints. It is the culture of us, the American people, that sets the precedent, and no simple election can truly alter our path, can shift our inner beliefs that lie deep within our cognitive processes. We are like clay; half-molded by our family and genetics, half-molded by societal standards, and both family and society are influenced by one another. And these morals stem far beyond what our stereotypical views of high morality infer; what the individual with high morals behaves like: Staying away from drugs, using appropriate manners, opening the door for others, saying 'please' and 'thank you', avoiding the excessive use of cuss words, donating, volunteering, displaying cooperative qualities etc. This isn't simply an alteration of morality which has generated more people who cuss, or do not open the door for others, or fail to use appropriate manners; it is the generation of values which demean those who open the door for others in the name of sexism, the generation of people who contract STDs, become rape victims or rapists, and undergo multiple abortions due to their excessive lack of appropriate manners; manners that society allows, and in many cases, encourages. It is the toleration of values which endanger others, and the intolerance of traditional values which have implanted America's foundation. Simple proper behavior is the least of the concern.

For example: The people that we as citizens place in the realms of popularity, rather than the media, effectively reflect the general moral standards of our society. A teenager, who is described in a Dr. Phil website entry as "I Want To Give Up My Car-Stealing, Knife-Wielding, Twerking 13-Year-Old Daughter Who Tried To Frame Me For A Crime", infamously known for the "*Cash me outside, howbow dah?*" phrase, managed to accumulate over 151,000 followers on Twitter.[10/11] In contrast, Kyle Carpenter, retired US marine and Medal of Honor recipient (The highest medal possibly awarded by the US military) only yields a fourth of that count.[9] A poorly-structured sentence placed Danielle Peskowitz Bregoli in the realms of popularity, which is indicative as to how little it takes in order to achieve fame in modern society. Instead of exalting individuals like Justin Bieber, known for basically abusing his fans and driving under the influence, or Farrah Abraham, who achieved celebrity status by starring on MTV's *Teen Mom*, or Kim Kardashian, one of the highest-earning reality television stars on earth because of her marriage with Kanye West and producing a sex video,[12] maybe we should direct more recognition and attention towards people like Maya Varma; an eighteen-year-old who invented a device which can diagnose chronic lung diseases such as asthma and emphysema by utilizing only $35 worth of electronic components,[13] or Dr Bon Verweij; a neurosurgeon who was the first to successfully transplant a full 3D-printed skull.[14] These people make meaningful and essential contributions to our world, yet oftentimes their recognition is overshadowed by the drama which circulates around Hollywood, and the American people can't get enough of it.

The people who we idolize can impact other detrimental areas of moral deterioration. For instance, the rising popularity of sexual deviants such as Kim Kardashian and Farrah Abraham are also rising with an increased rate of inappropriate sexual activity. The rate of contracting sexually transmitted diseases has reached an all-time high, according to the Centers for Disease Control and

Prevention. Since 2014, cases of Syphilis rose by 19%, Gonorrhea by 12.8%, and Chlamydia by 5.9% nationwide.[4] In relation with the increasing numbers of STD cases, an estimated one in ten people will be sexually abused before their 18th birthday.[6] And partly thanks to TV shows like *16 and Pregnant*, the United States has the highest rate of teen pregnancies and teen abortions in the developed world.[5] But celebrity influence is not the only possible culprit; other aspects could include the unusually short sentencing regulations for first-time convicted child molesters. According to a study by the Washington State Institute for Public Policy, "The average length of stay in prison is 60 months for offenders convicted of sex crimes against adults, 44 months for offenders convicted of sex crimes against children, and 33 months for all other sex offenders."[8] Combine that will other experiments that seemingly subdue the severity of child pedophilia, such as a new 'tactic' being developed by Trottla, a company that creates sex-dolls to gratify the desires of pedophiles. The owner, Shin Takagi, told The Atlantic that "I am helping people express their desires, legally and ethically."[7] Would this actually help alleviate those desires, or is it indicative that we as a society are gradually increasing our tolerance towards child molesters, rapists, and pedophiles? Tolerance is fine, if directed towards appropriate acts such as homosexuality, gender, and ethnicity. But molestation is heading down a twisted, dangerous path that could easily lead to more victims of sexual abuse. The influence of the famous, the laws we produce, and our general underestimation of the severity of these conditions, practically inhibit our ability to fix them.

Unlike several other topics discussed in this book, our deep cultural and societal values cannot be altered by simply electing different people into power, or even a different political party. Republicans undeniably control the US government at this point; the House, Senate, and Presidency, but the implementation of Conservative ideals into modern society is virtually impossible. And despite being representatives; being idealistically upstanding individuals who encompass the concept of a model citizen, the reality of modern politics is far from the theory. Moral standards most certainly can't be assisted by those in office, especially when those standards have infected the minds of the representatives themselves. Mud-slinging, bribery, and manipulation has never been more obvious than during the 2016 presidential election. Hillary Clinton calling half of Trump's supporters "A basket of deplorables". Donald Trump claiming that John McCain was "...not a war hero. He was a war hero because he was captured. I like people who weren't captured." Marco Rubio mocking Trump by stating "...have you seen his (Trump's) hands? And you know what they say about men with small hands..." And it still continues even after the election.[15] Top Democrats refusing to stand for Trump's honoring of slain Navy SEAL Ryan Owens.[16] SNL writer Katie Rich tweeting that Donald Trump's son "...will be this country's first homeschool shooter."[17] Hillary Clinton calling for "resistance and persistence" by the Democratic Party against the Trump administration.[18] Politics has always been considered a dirty, nasty power-struggle endeavor, but the immaturity and less-than-apprehensible behavior continues to worsen every election cycle.

The representatives of this nation carry the same influential weight as celebrities. They are often idolized, revered, glorified; their actions followed closely by the media. Politicians most often act in accordance with the general behavior of society, so that they can acquire more support, and therefore, more votes from the public. If Mrs. Clinton feels the need to deploy a derogatory rapper to gain more support, then that behavior reflects the general behavior of her supporters. While celebrities have the freedom to behave in any way they choose, politicians are more reliant on the support of the population; therefore, they often mimic societal beliefs and values. If the savagery in the political universe continues to worsen, then society is partially to blame due to its increasing acceptance towards otherwise inappropriate behavior. And we as citizens also take up a portion of the blame. After all, it is our responsibility to elect the most qualified representatives, and if the actions of a certain politician appear vile, any informed citizen will know better than to vote for that individual. The success of politicians and celebrities alike are ultimately determined by the command of the citizens, so if the actions of both reflect a moral deprivation, then so too are we experiencing a moral deprivation.

If the morals of society are so deeply entrenched, so entangled in its inner-workings, then what can be done to alter the path? There is no one answer which can 'solve' this issue and the only true way to initiate any major changes must be a collective movement. Placing the proper people in the spotlight, electing morally sound politicians, showing intolerance towards obviously corrupt behavior (Pedophilia, beastiality, incest etc.), and most importantly, producing a value-rich, loving home environment are all ways to assist. According to a Pew Research Center analysis of American Community Survey (ACS) and Decennial Census data, only 46% of U.S. kids 18 years or younger are living in a home with two married, heterosexual parents in their first marriage; in 1960 it was 73%, and in 1980 61%.[19] The lack of proper family structure can produce detrimental effects on the children raised in those environments; if the child matures struggling, then that person is more likely to lead a more aggressive, unbalanced life. Traditionally, both parents play uniquely different-yet equally important roles in the development of a child's life. The mother displays the more nurturing component; teaching the child the ideals of caring and sympathy, while the father teaches the child how to survive and thrive; how to live and function independently. If one or both of these components are absent, then that has a negative effect on the child's life; if the child leads a subdued life, then those values are passed down to the next generation of offspring. The negativity continues a cyclical existence.

Society influences us; the media influences us; celebrities and politicians influence us; music, movies, television shows, and videogames influence us; our friends and peers influence us; genetics influence us. Every day we are influence by our environment, but none play as large of a role in shaping our moral identity as the very home we develop in. As children, our thoughts are fragile; we are easily manipulative. Almost like clay, we are permanently shaped by the environment we reside in, and most, if not all of the moral inconsistencies of the modern world can be solved if the proper values are instilled through our childhoods. But that is not easy. Providing a compelling argument to encourage stable families is nearly incomprehensible. Educating the population on the benefits of proper care-giving is a start, but this is a deeply-rooted issue, though not impossible. Because society influences us, it influences our families, and following through with the options previously listed can still guide families in the right direction. We have accomplished much in several areas of moral development, but we cannot allow the root of it to wither away; if one area advances, so should the rest.

# Chapter 12: Capitalism versus Socialism

Collectivism. Unity. Generosity. Equality. Nobody is poor; nobody is rich. No personal property; no greed. If you need something, then it is my duty to supply it. Nobody goes hungry; nobody perishes. Free healthcare; free birth control; free college; free food. In this economy, equality reigns supreme; everyone gets what they want, whenever they want it. A dystopian paradise. On the flip side, we discover greed. Corruption. Materialistic obsession. Corporatism. Individualism. A rat race to the top; a rat race where only the privileged win. Poverty. Selfishness. Discrimination. If you're starving, then it's your own fault. If you need something; get it yourself. An obvious disaster. One method has worked, and the other has failed. One method remains implanted into every developed nation's economy, while the other struggles to survive among nations riddled with poverty, inflation, and corruption.

Socialism, in essence, promises prosperity for every citizen. As stated by Vladimir Lenin, "Democracy is indispensable to Socialism." True freedom can only exist under a system of such enormous magnitudes of collectivism, according to Marxist philosophy.[1] It is an 'ideal' economic system which promised to eliminate several of the less-than-attractive instinctual characteristics of mankind; greed, selfishness, and jealousy. Socialism is comprised of a few key components which aid in identifying the system: There are no national borders or independent nations, no personal property (It is instead distributed among the population) or social classes (the process of narrowing the gap between the wealthy and impoverished classes), and the community controls the means of production (setting the prices for materials, and controlling the distribution and exportation of goods and services).[3] These characteristics were highly prevalent during the fledgling years of Socialist philosophy, spearheaded by Karl Marx and Friedrich Engels when they published *The Communist Manifesto* in 1848. Because of the founders, Marxist Socialism; the version of Socialism most closely related to Communism, was termed.[4]

Capitalism, on the other hand, is more commonly associated with the principles of our nation. Our current economic system encourages prosperity through achievement and entrepreneurship; the utilization of competition as a basis for success. Like Socialism, Capitalism can be easily summarized into a few primary components: The means of production is privately owned (Business owners determine the price and distribution of their goods), businesses are able (and encouraged) to freely compete with one another, limited government interference, and the laws of supply and demand play a major role (When supplies increase, prices tend to drop. If prices drop, demand generally increases until supplies deplete. Because of this, prices will rise again, but only as long as demand remains high) which, in theory, regulates prices from either getting too high or low.[2] The origins of Capitalism derive as early as the Middle Ages; lending money at interest; each merchant being essentially a Capitalist.[5] The modern version of the system, however, traces its roots to the Industrial Revolution, where concepts of individual employers hiring multiple employees accelerates into a widespread reality. Adam Smith, known as the father of Capitalism, brought the premises of Capitalism into light with the publication of his work *An Inquiry Into the Nature and Causes of the Wealth of Nations* in 1776.[6] This was when Capitalism became widely accepted as its own independent economic system.

But why even bother discussing these two systems; what underlying motive must possibly tie into current conditions? In recent years, the attractiveness of Socialism in Capitalist nations has been steadily growing. According to the results of a recent YouGov survey, where respondents were asked if they had either a favorable or unfavorable view of Socialism and Capitalism, the Democrat demographic rated both systems equally positive (42% favorability) while the 'Under 30' demographic rated Socialism *higher* than Capitalism (43% vs 32% favorability). Additionally, Gallup recently asked surveyors about whether they would be willing to vote for a well-qualified presidential candidate whom their party nominated, and who happened to be from a particular background (Gay, Catholic, Hispanic etc.), and the results among the youngest respondents remained favorable towards Socialism. While only 34 percent of respondents age 65 or older would be willing to vote for a Socialist, 69 percent of respondents in the 18 to 29 age range were willing to vote for a Socialist; giving the biggest differential of 35 percent (Youngest group minus oldest group) out of the eleven listed characteristics in the poll.[7] So if America's Millennials are becoming more supportive of Socialist philosophy, then they ought to know what the consequences are.

Karl Marx once stated "The history of all previous societies has been the history of class struggles."[9] History can be a highly effective tool in argument persuasion; it can be used to either validate or debunk one's ideas, because it provides factual examples. Individuals such as Karl Marx, Vladimir Lenin, and Fidel Castro have all pointed towards history as reinforcement for Socialism, but history provides numerous unique comparisons between the two economic systems; it does such an excellent job that these examples could be considered textbook-quality side-by-side comparisons between Capitalism and Socialism/Communism, and the results are one-sided to say the least.

After World War 2, the entire country of Germany was divided into two separate entities; The Federal Republic of Germany (West Germany), run by the Allies, and the German Democratic Republic (East Germany), operated by the Soviet Union. Given the location and importance of Berlin, Germany's capital, it too was split between the Capitalists and Communists. The side which the residents of the city preferred was not arguable; the eventual creation of the Berlin Wall in 1961-66 miles of concrete; 3.6 meters high with 41 miles of barbed wire and over 300 manned watchtowers, was to prevent the mass-exodus of East Berliners into West Berlin-2.5 million since the split originally formed in 1949. Despite the heavily-guarded and fortified walls, an estimated 5,000 people-including 1300 guards, managed to escape by climbing the walls, and roughly 200 perished during failed attempts.[8] How severe must an economy be for people to risk even death? How treacherous and abysmal must conditions be for such large quantities of people to venture the possibility of the extinction of life itself; is getting shot in the head and buried under a shallow grave worth it? To those living in East Berlin, the answer was yes. Capitalism 1, Communism 0.

The creation of the Berlin Wall occurred during a more global conflict between Capitalism and Communism-the Cold War. Yet another ideal example of the inefficiencies of Communism and Socialist philosophy, a major factor of America's victory was not due to our capabilities, but rather the economy of the Soviet Union. Russia's government controlled the means of production; basically, they had to supply nourishment for its people, as well as maintain a military buildup to rival the United States. By the 1980's, seventy percent of Russia's industrial output went straight to the military-depleting the other federal programs, but problems began to arise far before. One such issue, according to one anonymous Soviet Citizen, was that "They pretend to pay us and we pretend to work." This was due to the lack of incentives for productivity; the workers did not want to work. Why? Perhaps it is due to the lack of success or advancement one acquires under a Communist system. Working harder or more diligently than your fellow comrade was, essentially, a waste of effort. Grigory Yavlinsky, a Russian economist and top advisor to Mikhail Gorbachev, highlights this issue when he states "The Soviet system is not working because the workers are not working."[10] With the increased wealth that our Capitalist system was able to produce, the United States was able to maintain a powerful military while simultaneously being able to provide for its citizens. The Soviet Union simply was incapable of investing large quantities of income into their military while trying to fight their extreme poverty rates, which exceeded twenty percent by 1989.[11] It is no wonder that our nation emerged victorious, and why Russia's economy has turned more Capitalistic with Perestroika. Capitalism 2, Communism 0.

Even today, examples still exist of the contrasts between Capitalism and Communism, such as North and South Korea. Here a few statistics contrasting the two countries: North Korea's GDP per capita is ranked 197th in the world-South Korea's GDP is 18 times higher. Approximately half of North Korea's population lives in 'extreme poverty', while the poverty rate in South Korea is 14.6 percent (In 2013), which is lower than several developed nations. The average life expectancy in North Korea is 69 years, which has fallen by five years since the 1980's.[12] On the other hand, one mathematical study-a blend of 21 separate forecasts, concluded that South Korean women will be the first in the world to achieve the average life expectancy of 90; currently, the overall average is 81.37 years.[14] According to the World Food Program, one-third of North Korean children are stunted due to malnutrition. Inflation in North Korea is roughly 100 percent, and most North Korean homes are heated by fire-places, rather than by electricity like in South Korea and the rest of the developed world.[12] It is difficult to believe how such oppositely-structured nations can even exist next to one another; one an industrial, democratic, technological powerhouse with a high standard of living, and the other an abysmal disaster. The government is so powerful and restrictive in North Korea, that they own the internet, media, healthcare, and employment. Information rarely travels into or out of the country, and the State constantly keeps their citizens ignorant by restricting their ability to access outside information, because if they could, the citizens would quickly realize just how disastrous their home truly is. The difference is clear. Capitalism 3, Communism 0.

But these are generally not the nations that the left alludes towards to justify Socialism. European nations, Australia, and Canada are common leverages in debates, yet is life truly bliss in these areas? Are these areas *actually* even Socialist? A deeper analysis provides a different alternative. In Denmark, for example, the income tax rate is 60.2 percent, which applies for incomes over $55,000. In comparison, the income tax rate for incomes over $400,000 in California (The state with the highest tax rates) is 47.6 percent. Denmark's sales tax rate is also significantly greater than the United States' rate-25 percent versus the 7.25 percent general sales tax rate in California, and Denmark has a catastrophic 180% new car tax.[16/19] Several other European nations such as Sweden and Norway have similar tax rates, but of course the argument now leads to the question: Are the tax rates worth it for the benefits?

One such benefit is free healthcare, or in professional terms, Single-Payer healthcare. Canada is a common nation that liberals tend to allude to as having a 'superior' healthcare system compared to the US, and therefore, we ought to design our system based upon that philosophy. Yet the United States already *has* a form of Single-Payer healthcare: The US Department of Veteran's Affairs (Commonly known as the VA). This system was implemented to care for our nation's veterans, yet our veterans have experienced first-hand all the problems associated with government healthcare. The VA is the second largest department in the federal government-containing over 340,000 employees, holding approximately 7 million patients, and receiving an annual budget of $180 billion; so we have already implemented Single-Payer healthcare on a larger scale. In Phoenix, Arizona in 2014, roughly 1,700 VA patients were forced to wait an average of 115 days for an appointment; yet the official VA policy states that patients should not be forced to wait longer than 14 days. Nationwide the corruption continued. In Fort Collins, Colorado, clerks were mandated to falsify records in order to perpetrate the illusion that VA doctors were seeing more patients than they actually were.[17] Despite a $1 million grant by the federal government for use in reducing delays; The VA in Columbia, South Carolina contained nearly 4,000 delays in cancer treatment-killing up to 20 veterans who died of the disease. Dr. Stephen Lloyd, a private physician specializing in colonoscopy in Columbia, commented on the situation by stating "(Veterans) paid the ultimate price. People that had appointments had their appointments canceled and rescheduled much later. ... In some cases, that made an impact where they went into a later stage (of illness) and therefore lost the battle to live."[18] In Pittsburgh, Pennsylvania, there was an outbreak of Legionnaires' Disease; government officials were aware of this disease, and waited over a year before releasing that information to the public; roughly six veterans died as a result.

Since 2009, the VA budget has nearly doubled, and they hired over 100,000 new employees in the past decade. Yet despite these actions, waiting times have continued to increase. Perhaps this is why 2/3 of our nation's veterans don't use the VA, while those that do acquire 75% of their healthcare from private healthcare facilities.[17] Even the luxurious Canada is experiencing similar calamities with their government healthcare. The Fraser Institute, a Canadian public policy think tank, estimates that 52,513 Canadians received non-emergency medical treatment outside of Canada in 2014; a 25 percent increase from the roughly 41,838 who sought medical care abroad the previous year.[21] The Commonwealth Fund, a U.S. think tank, released a report in 2014 ranking Canada 10th out of 11 wealthy nations in terms of health care; in terms of the timeliness of care, Canada ranked last.[20] Overall, the average Canadian family pays approximately $12,000 annually for their 'free' healthcare, according to the Fraser Institute.[22] It is no wonder why Americans have generally discarded the idea of Single-Payer healthcare; we've experienced it for ourselves, and our neighbors have shown us the reality of their system. America's veterans deserve a more superior system.

      This leads to yet another important question about the other Socialist nations of the developed world; are they actually even Socialist? While Canada, Sweden, Norway, Australia, Denmark, and several other developed countries have higher tax rates and regulations than the US, these Socialist ideals have been steadily decreasing in recent times. For instance, the top income tax rate in Scandinavian countries averages at around 50 percent; while high, this is a roughly 20 percent decrease from the previous 70 percent tax rate. The capital gains tax rate has also been cut to around 30 percent in European countries; not far off from the 22 percent rate in the United States. Denmark, in particular, is known for having one of the least regulated labor markets in Europe; their 'flexicurity' model.[24] Denmark's Prime Minister, Lars Lokke Rasmussen, made the declaration "I would like to make one thing clear: Denmark is far from a socialist planned economy; Denmark is a market economy."[19] Apparently, he was so fed up with Liberal Americans alluding to Denmark as being Socialist, that the clarification had to be made. Germany just recently established a minimum wage in

2015,[23] and Canada has a highly-selective immigration policy; applicants are rated-and accepted by their skills and adaptability to the Canadian workforce; a stark contrast from the open-border policies that many Americans support.[25] If you'd rather examine current nations that are *actually* Socialist, then look no further than to Venezuela, whose economy is in disarray.

It is easy to make the assumption that Capitalism is a greedy economic policy; individuals pursuing their own goals without a consideration for others. Yet is it not greedy to take the earnings of an individual without earning it yourself? Is it not greedy to believe that you are 'entitled' to reap the benefits of others; that you are 'entitled' to free healthcare, paid vacations, free college, free birth control, and free government benefits? In 2010, then-President Barack Obama addressed an eager crowd of college students, in which he announced "Young people will now be able to remain on their parents' health insurance plan until age 26." The applause which followed was thunderous; it must have made them so happy to know that they can successfully mooch off of their parents until well-into adulthood. And if one believes that one is *entitled* to certain benefits, then the whole concept of gratitude is discarded, because why say 'thank you' to something that you *deserve*? In the words of Dennis Prager, "Capitalism teaches people to work more; Socialism teaches people to demand more."[26] Want free college? Pay for it through the military or through scholarships. Want free healthcare? Do your research and purchase an affordable health care plan. Want multiple paid vacations? Earn it through your diligence as a worker. For those that *truly* need assistance, programs are available. Socialism encourages selfishness; Capitalism is reality.

# Chapter 13: Feminism: Is it Necessary?

To all of the females reading this book; do you believe that you are being oppressed? Do you believe that your gender is preventing you from achieving the same prospects as men? According to Progressive propaganda, you most certainly are, whether you realize it or not. You are a victim of the male hierarchy; you are paid less than your male peers; you do not receive the same rights, benefits, and freedoms that men are allowed to enjoy; society treats you as subhuman by the limitations they impose on you. There is no hope; no way out. Nothing can help you achieve what you so rightfully deserve-nothing except Feminism. That's right. Feminism can save you from the vicious grip of male privilege. Feminism cares for all women. Feminism is not biased or discriminatory; instead, it is selfless and kind. Let us embrace your struggles, your hardships. (And don't you dare say you have none-you're a woman; trust us, you're definitely oppressed) Welcome to the world of first-world Feminism.

Pursuing equal rights for all is an admirable act, and it is one which the world can one day universally accept. Equality, however, is distant from special privileges; it demands equal treatment for *all* sides. The United States was once a nation where equal rights were anything but equal; women and minorities were treated as second-class citizens for the majority of our nation's' existence. The inability to own private property, the inability to vote, to hold office, to be elected, to receive an education, or to even use the same drinking fountain as a white person were once realities. Once. We have astronomically improved our position on equal rights since that era, and in some cases, our apologies have gone too far (As detailed in chapter 7). Compared with the rest of the world, women and minorities are treated the best here; our immense diversity is proof of that claim. Yet are we truly equal? If we are, then why do groups such as Black Lives Matter and ideas such as feminism continue to exist and thrive? The third-wave feminist believes that despite our nation's advances in equality, we still have much work to do. They often cite the supposed wage gap between men and women; how they are forced to pay for birth control; the rape culture; how they can't show their breasts in public (That's right. The 'Free the Nipple' movement is actually a thing). Yet how accurate are these accusations? I've done this kind of rhetorical question long enough to where you know the answer: Not accurate at all.

Let's start with the wage gap; an idea being falsely spread by the media and politicians like wildfire. Women make 77 cents of the dollar compared with men; calculated by dividing the median earnings of all women working full-time by the median earnings of all men working full time. Sounds like solidified proof that the wage gap exists, right? Hardly. The wage gap, in reality, is one of the most misleading claims in the modern world. The 77 cent equation does not take occupation, position, or education into account; the results change drastically when these are taken into consideration. The American Association of University Women, a feminist organization, conducted a study which revealed that the wage gap shrinks to just 6.6 cents after factoring the different choices men and women make. The 6.6 can be narrowed to 0 when factoring in individual occupational choices between the sexes. The US Department of Labor examined over 50 peer-reviewed studies; they concluded that the .23 cent wage gap is almost entirely the result of individual choices that men and women make, not the result of sexism. So let's narrow down exactly what occupational choices women make versus men which has determined this wage gap. Georgetown University once compiled a list of the 5 best paying college majors, along with the percentage of men and women majoring in those fields. Petroleum Engineering-87% male. Mathematics and Computer Science-67% male. Aerospace Engineering-88% male. Chemical Engineering-72% male. Women only out-represent men in just one; Pharmaceutical Sciences-48% male. They also conducted a study of the 5 worst-paying majors. Counseling and Psychology-74% female. Early Childhood Education-97% female. Human Services and Community Organization-81% female. Social Work-88% female. Men only out-represented women in just one; Theology and Religious vocations-66% male.

Yet some will still point out the wage gap between the sexes who major in the same fields. Take nursing for instance; male nurses, on average, make 18% more than their female counterparts. The reason? Male nurses are more likely to work longer hours, gravitate to the best-paying specialty, and often relocate to better-paying areas. Professor Linda Aiken of the University of Pennsylvania comments by stating "...Career choices and educational differences explain most, if not all, the gender gap in nursing." Simply put, women are more likely to gravitate towards jobs that are generally not as stressful and offer more free-time (Perhaps to care for their children); men, however, tend to gravitate towards the best-paying jobs.[1] We love making money. Even if all the previously-stated evidence was false, if the wage gap was truly the result of sexism, it would be *illegal*. The Equal Pay Act of 1963 was implemented for this very reason, which clearly states "No employer having employees subject to any provisions of this section shall discriminate, within any establishment in which such employees are employed, between employees on the basis of sex by paying wages to employees in such establishment at a rate less than the rate at which he pays wages to employees of the opposite sex..."[5] If businesses could get away with paying women less, why wouldn't they only try to hire them? The wage gap is not a myth; it is a myth when tied with sexism and discrimination.

Another question boggling the minds of American feminists is why they have to conceal their breasts while men do not. How awful, not being able to reveal your boobs in public. The answer is rather simple: Men's nipples produce no sexual effect, while women's breasts do. According to the results of MRI images, three sensory maps of the parietal cortex light up when female genitalia is (self) stimulated; one represents the clitoris, another the vagina, and the last one the cervix. All three of these light up when the female nipple is stimulated, providing a source of sexual pleasure for women; this also means that female breasts double as a sexual organ-for both men and women.[12] Arguably, a woman displaying her breasts in public is no different than a man displaying his penis, which is also not allowed. In terms of birth control; part of being independent involves paying for things yourself. In terms of the 'Rape culture', nobody is advocating rape. This is where concealed carry comes in handy.

These kinds of complaints are the kind women in other areas of the world *wished* they had to only deal with. In Iran, women are forbidden from watching men's sports, and married women cannot leave the country without their husband's permission.[3] In 2015, Saudi Arabian women were finally allowed to vote for the first time, and only recently were they allowed to even drive.[4] A 2010 report from the Freedom House found that in 2009, political rights and civil liberties declined globally for the fourth consecutive year with the MENA (Middle East and North Africa) region achieving last place. Currently, 88% of the population there resides in countries that are 'Not Free'; they lack basic democratic institutions which stagnate women's rights progress.[2] While the situation in the United States may not be perfect, the problems women face here are infinitesimal compared with the problems of other nations-particularly in the MENA region. There, the patriarchy has near-complete control of the lives of the women; a man must accompany you whenever you leave the house; a man must give you permission to leave the country; a man forces you to conceal yourself from head to toe in public; a man tells you what to do, when to do it, and where to do it. There, you're not a human being; you're an object-a toy, a slave. And here you are stressing about not being able to flaunt your boobs in public.

Even here in the states, men don't always get the lenient side of the deal. In numerous areas, women gain the upper hand; arguably 'special privileges' that equality-toting feminists are perfectly content with. In 2015, men accounted for 92.4 percent of occupational fatalities-4,454 male deaths versus 367 female deaths.[6] During Operation Iraqi Freedom (March 19, 2003 through

May 3, 2008), men accounted for 97.68 percent of military deaths.[10] Men are 3.5 times more likely to die from suicide than women,[7] and men accounted for the majority of murder victims in 2010 at 77.4 percent.[8] Between 1993 and 2007, women, on average, had a 84 percent chance of winning child custody in court, and women have a roughly 20 percent increased chance over men in receiving child support.[9] Men are forced to sign up for a draft; male rape victims are laughed at rather than comforted; men face societal scrutiny to 'man up' during times of emotional stress; men are less likely to receive benefits from the government. Honestly, if you're a white male, your chances of receiving financial aid are minimal at best.

The modern feminist also claims to be a champion for *all* women, yet how truthful is that? In January of 2017, an Anti-Trump Women's March ascended upon Washington, and a pro-life group, the New Wave Feminists, wished to join them; they, too, were aggravated by Trump's comments about women on the campaign trail. The Women's March banned the pro-lifers from joining after leftist feminists voiced their outrage. "Intersectional feminism does not include a pro-life agenda. That's not how it works! The right to choose is a fundamental part of feminism." feminist Roxane Gay wrote on Twitter. "Horrified that the @womensmarch has partnered w/an anti-choice org. Plse reconsider- inclusivity is not about bolstering those who harm us," Jessica Valenti also commented.[11] According to the philosophy of the Liberal feminist, one can only be a feminist if they are pro-choice. In a situation like this, since both groups were marching for the same reason, wouldn't the right thing be to set aside the differences between the groups in order to march under one noble cause? Of course not. The modern feminist is exclusive, not inclusive, towards dissenting opinions of other women. We will only support you if your beliefs are identical with ours. That is the Liberal way; that is the feminist way.

As feminism continues to seep through our culture, especially since icons like Beyoncé, Emma Watson, Miley Cyrus, Oprah, and Lena Dunham have revealed their feminist beliefs; the spread of exclusion and favoritism; entitlement and narcissism that tends to tag along with modern feminism will also continue to spread. Even brands have hopped on the bandwagon. Under Armour's "I Will What I Want" campaign celebrates the work of ballerina Misty Copeland, who was told she had the "wrong body" for ballet. Dove's "Real Beauty Sketches" told women they're more beautiful than they think. And Always' #LikeAGirl ad alluded to female stereotypes; as defined by moderator Samantha Skey, Chief Revenue Officer of SheKnows, this type of advertising is called "femvertising".[13] Of course, telling women to be empowering is not damaging; it is noble, if the companies are sincere about their intentions, anyways. It is certainly possible that some companies have simply manipulated the trendiness of feminism to more effectively sell their products, which is reflective of how popular feminism has become. Recently, it has been losing some steam. Why? Perhaps because more women are beginning to realize that their life isn't quite so bad here in the states.

Feminism, in essence, is not necessarily bad. During the era of its creation, it was necessary; it was vital and crucial for the advancement of women's rights. Even today, some areas of the world are in desperate need of feminism (Maybe more feminists here could help them out). Today, however, in which I will declare with my utmost honesty, feminism is no longer needed in the United States. At this point, to demand more would be surpassing the point of equality and would be heading towards favoritism. That was not the original purpose of Feminism. Feminism used to stress equality for all, though today you'd be an egalitarian rather than a feminist to still support equality. To the women who are reading this: You are *not* oppressed. You are *not* treated as a second-class citizen. You *do* enjoy the same rights as everyone else. You *can* be proud of women's advancements in our nation thanks to strong, determined women who have fought for equality with blood, sweat, and tears, and they have *achieved* that goal. The modern feminist will keep arguing that you're a victim. If anything, *that's* sexist and demeaning, because as a woman living in the United States, you're not a victim to *anybody*, and you don't blame anyone else for your problems. American Feminism needs you more than you need it; it feeds off of fear and blaming others to survive. Let it die out.

# *Chapter 14*: Our Future

Without exception, the United States is the greatest nation to ever exist. Ever since our creation, it has been the American way to challenge the status quo of the era, beginning with a neat little experiment known as Democracy. Historically and currently, we have been regarded as the beacon of hope; the shining city on the hill for the weary, the tired, the sick, the oppressed, and the ridiculed. We are exceptional. We are constantly pushing to improve ourselves. We strive to continue our status as a land of opportunity. We are the most diverse nation on the planet; it is not surprising why that is so. We have always prided ourselves in our uniqueness compared with the rest of the world, because our differences have accelerated our nation to be the best-economically, militarily, with our freedoms and our liberties.

But a change is on the horizon; a change that threatens to abandon our values as a nation, the values of our Founding Fathers. It cannot be stopped by a simple election or a transfer of political power. This change threatens to change the very identity of the United States; politically, economically, militarily, and morally. If we are to continue being exceptional; if we are to continue being the greatest in the world, then it is imperative that we retain our values of independence, work ethic, morality, and liberties. Our speech is being silenced, government dependency is being encouraged, and our Judeo-Christian values our being degraded, all under the radar; in secrecy, and sometimes right in the open, because we are doing little to stop it. The very countries that we have fought with blood, sweat, and tears against to separate ourselves from their ideologies, are becoming those very same countries that we are attempting to model ourselves after.

Much has occurred during the 2-year span of writing this book. More examples of Political Correctness in our schools and facilities; more examples of college indoctrination; more examples of gun restrictions and failed policies; more examples of technological dependency. With our new president and Republican majority in the House and Senate, it is easy to now disregard some of my chapters; President Trump has already reversed many of the international policies of the Obama Administration by bombing Syria with cruise missiles and dropping a MOAB in Afghanistan. These are positive changes that I applaud, but chapter 10 remains relevant. Identifying where we went wrong in order to prevent those same cataclysms is the sole purpose of studying history, right? I understand the Obama Administration is over; I understand that Clinton didn't win the presidency, but our culture is still gradually transforming into a more progressive one. The people who voted in President Trump will not last forever; soon, the millennials will replace them as the majority voting population, and soon, their values will be the ones elected into office.

Much more will occur after writing these last few paragraphs; some in favor of my arguments, some against. The negative stories are a constant flow; a stream which the mainstream media is dependent on for nourishment. Considering the world we live in, the stream won't stop. It never stops. Its ferocity is ever-growing, and no barrier or dam can halt its progress. We can try all we might; ignore the negativity, but it's still there nevertheless. There are many more chapters I could have written about: the War on Christianity, the

Environment, National Security, or Islamic Cultural Influence. These problems are still in the fledgling stages; they will worsen, and they will grow more severe in the upcoming years. I am certain that my Christian faith will one-day be put to the test. Incidents of rape and sexual abuse are increasing in Europe with the new flood of Muslim immigrants. A culture clash is on the horizon, but it has yet to reveal itself here, at least not yet. And believe me; Trump being president won't make a difference. The worst has yet to come.

So what can we do to prevent such a catastrophe? For one, we must apologetically remain firm in our national values. We *cannot* allow the values of MENA immigrants to alter ours; they came to our country out of their own free will, and they ought to either accept our beliefs or leave. Second, we need to quickly and assuredly halt the degradation of our values here at home. Let people wave the American flag, let people voice their opinions at our colleges and schools, let people retain their rights to own firearms. Educate people about the dangers of Socialism, educate people about the dangers of technological dependency, and educate people about the dangers of moral, international, educational, and moral decay. As Ronald Reagan once stated at the Brandenburg Gate in 1987 "I have read, and I have been questioned since I've been here about certain demonstrations against my coming. And I would like to say just one thing, and to those who demonstrate so. I wonder if they have ever asked themselves that if they should have the kind of government they apparently seek, no one would ever be able to do what they're doing again."[1] The majority of our problems can be solved through education; too many people have no clue what is happening around them, and it is a recipe for disaster.

I wrote this book because Millennials tend to only listen to other Millennials (Or in my case Generation Z if you want to get technical). It is a warning to our youth; the people of our future. I don't know if this book will make a difference; I don't know if the whole thing was just a waste of time. My knowledge has expanded considerably during my writing; I received just as much of an education through writing this piece as anyone who may read it. I worry for the future of this nation. We are great, and we must remain great. Our generation will experience the largest wave of change compared with any other in history; that, I am certain of. This is our time. We have the ability to continue being that beacon of hope, but it must be supported. This is our generation to take control of.

# *Appendix*

## Age of Technology

1. Evans, Heidi. "Toddlers may be at risk from technology, warn experts as new study shows use soars by diaper set." New York Daily News, 7 Apr. 2014. Web.

2. Richter, Felix. "Americans Use Electronic Media 11 Hours A Day." *Statista.* N.p., 13 Mar. 2015. Web.

3. "Hard Disk Drive Morph." *Processing Power Compared.* N.p., n.d. Web. <http://pages.experts-exchange.com/processing-power-compared/>.

4. White, Charlie. "Smartphones leave yesterday's supercomputers in the dust ." N.p., Sept. & oct. 2013. Web. <http://www.charliewhite.net/2013/09/smartphones-vs-supercomputers/>.

5. Staff, Investopedia. "Moore's Law." *Investopedia.* N.p., 24 Nov. 2003. Web.

6. "Ten of the coolest and most powerful supercomputers of all time." *Pingdom Royal.* N.p., 11 June 2009. Web.

7. Neuman, Scott. "Obama Orders Development Of Supercomputer To Rival China's 'Milky Way'" *NPR.* NPR, 30 July 2015. Web.

8. Smith, Aaron. "U.S. Smartphone Use in 2015." *Pew Research Center: Internet, Science & Tech.* N.p., 01 Apr. 2015. Web.

9.  Aquino, Judith. "Nine jobs that humans may lose to robots."nbcnews.com NBCUniversal News Group, 22 Mar. 2011. Web.

10. Rowan, Cris. "Moving to Learn." *Insights from a leading child-development expert.* N.p., 8 June 2013. Web.

11. TopTenSM Staff. "10 pros and cons of social media." *Top Ten Social Media.* N.p., n.d. Web.

12. Satell, Greg. "What Can We Expect From The Next Decade of Technology?" *Forbes.* Forbes Magazine, 07 July 2013. Web.

13. "The Emerging Future is twice as good." *Estimating the Speed of Exponential Technological Advancement, The emerging Future.* N.p., n.d. Web. <http://theemergingfuture.com/speed-technological-advancement.htm>.

14. Kennon, Tammy. "5 new brain disorders that were born out of the digital age." *The Week - All you need to know about everything that matters.* N.p., 28 Feb. 2017. Web.

15. Stewart, Will. "Could we bring the woolly mammoth back to life? Scientists say they have reached milestone in efforts to clone the hairy beast." *Daily Mail Online.* Associated Newspapers, 29 July 2016. Web.

16. "Cloning Fact Sheet." *National Human Genome Research Institute (NHGRI).* N.p., n.d. Web. <https://www.genome.gov/25020028/cloning-fact-sheet/>.

# Political Correctness

1. Kiriyama, George. "Students Kicked Off Campus for Wearing American Flag Tees." *NBC Bay Area*. NBC Bay Area, 29 Sept. 2010. Web.

2. Starnes, Todd. "School Orders Child to Remove God From Poem." *Fox News*. FOX News Network, 29 Nov. 2012. Web.

3. <http://www.examiner.com/article/msnbc-saying-golf-and-chicago-is-racist>

4. Chasmar, Jessica. "Stevenson College apologizes for serving Mexican food at alien-themed party." *The Washington Times*. The Washington Times, 17 Apr. 2015. Web.

5. Soave, Robby. "The University of California's Insane Speech Police." *The Daily Beast*. The Daily Beast Company, 22 June 2015. Web.

6. Kaminer, Wendy. "The progressive ideas behind the lack of free speech on campus." *The Washington Post*. WP Company, 20 Feb. 2015. Web.

7. Wold, Nathan. "10 Most Absurd Things Banned On Politically Correct College Campuses." *Listverse*. N.p., 25 Aug. 2015. Web.

8. Chumley, Cheryl K. "Al Jazeera English bans words: 'Terrorist,' 'Islamist,' 'jihad' off-limits to news employees." *The Washington Times*. The Washington Times, 28 Jan. 2015. Web.

9. Richter, Greg. "Al Jazeera Video Mocks Americans as Fat, Racist, Violent." *Newsmax*. N.p., 05 July 2015. Web.

10. Hebert, Brady. "Cheboygan schools update Chiefs logo." *Cheboygan Daily Tribune*. Cheboygan Daily Tribune - Cheboygan, MI, 11 Nov. 2014. Web.

11. Melber, Ari. "Legal Scholar: Trump's Muslim Ban May Be Constitutional."nbcnews.com NBCUniversal News Group, 23 Dec. 2015. Web.

12. Stanglin, Doug. "Purported terrorist recruitment video includes Donald Trump clip." *USA Today*. Gannett Satellite Information Network, 02 Jan. 2016. Web.

## The Indoctrination

1. Riddell, Kelly. "99% of top liberal arts professor campaign donations go to Democrats: report." *The Washington Times*. The Washington Times, 27 Oct. 2015. Web.

2. Johnson, Natalie. "Liberal Professors Outnumber Conservative Faculty 5 to 1. Academics Explain Why This Matters." *Amac*. N.p., 22 Jan. 2016. Web.

3. <http://www.iop.harvard.edu/media-bias-alive-and-well>

4. Perazzo, John. "Research On Media Bias." *Research on Media Bias - Discover the Networks*. N.p., 31 Oct. 2008. Web.

## Vanishing Traditions

1. Westcott, Lucy, James Somers, Franklin Foer, Tara García Mathewson, David A. Graham, Jerry Useem, Ed Yong, Rob Walker, Olga Khazan, Phoebe Maltz Bovy, Amanda Gefter, Katherine Wells, Jackie Lay, Ta-Nehisi Coates, and Daniel

Lombroso. "More Americans Moving to Cities, Reversing the Suburban Exodus." *The Atlantic*. N.p., 27 Mar. 2014. Web.

2. CBSNews. "Number Of Hunters In U.S. Declining." *CBS News*. CBS Interactive, 03 Sept. 2007. Web.

3. Wardle, Lynn. "The American Family: An Endangered and Disappearing Species." *CNS News*. N.p., 16 June 2015. Web.

## Gun Control

1. Reporter, IBT Staff. "Colorado Massacre: Are Americans The Most Heavily Armed People On The Planet?" *International Business Times*. N.p., 26 July 2012. Web.

2. "American Hunters – The World's Largest Army." *Fox News*. FOX News Network, 04 Nov. 2013. Web.

3. Koba, Mark. "U.S. Military Spending Dwarfs Rest of World."nbcnews.com NBCUniversal News Group, 24 Feb. 2014. Web.

4. Hookstead, David. "Hillary Clinton Blames NRA For Mass Shootings." *The Daily Caller*. N.p., 2 Oct. 2015. Web.

5. Hawkins, Awr. "Report: 92 Percent of Mass Shootings Since 2009 Occurred in Gun-Free Zones." *Breitbart*. N.p., 11 Oct. 2014. Web.

6. Rucker, Philip, and Abby Phillip. "Clinton and allies attack Sanders on gun control ahead of N.Y. primary." *The Washington Post*. WP Company, 11 Apr. 2016. Web.

7.  Berman, Mark. "Chicago's staggering rise in gun violence and killings." *The Washington Post*. WP Company, 02 Apr. 2016. Web.

8.  Nolan, Steve. "25 Reasons Why We Need to Preserve Our 2nd Amendment Right to Keep and Bear Arms." *Activist Post*. N.p., 12 Aug. 2015. Web.

9.  Phillips, Amber. "The gun-control debate, explained in 5 questions." *The Washington Post*. WP Company, 03 Dec. 2015. Web.

10. Farley, Robert. "Gun Rhetoric vs. Gun Facts." *FactCheck.org*. N.p., 21 Dec. 2012. Web.

## Prejudice: A Two-Way Street

1.  "Martin Luther King I Have a Dream Speech." *American Rhetoric*. N.p., n.d. Web. <http://www.americanrhetoric.com/speeches/mlkihaveadream.htm>.

2.  "African Participation and Resistance to the Trade · African Passages, Lowcountry Adaptations." *Lowcountry Digital History Initiative*. N.p., n.d. Web. <http://ldhi.library.cofc.edu/exhibits/show/africanpassageslowcountryadapt/introductionatlanticworld/african_participation_and_resi>.

3.  Grabmeier, Jeff. "When Europeans Were Slaves: Research Suggests White Slavery Was Much More Common Than Previously Believed." *Ohio State Research*. N.p., 8 Mar. 2004. Web.

4.  Holloway, April. "The White Slaves of Barbary." *Ancient Origins*. Ancient Origins, n.d. Web.

5. "Pathways to Freedom | About the Underground Railroad." *Pathways to Freedom: Maryland and the Underground Railroad*. Maryland Public Television, n.d. Web. <http://pathways.thinkport.org/about/about6.cfm>.

6. Carr, Karen. "Chinese Slavery - Were there slaves in ancient China?" *Quatr.us*. N.p., n.d. Web.

7. "American Slavery in Comparative Perspective." *Digital History*. N.p., n.d. Web. <http://www.digitalhistory.uh.edu/disp_textbook.cfm?smtID=2&psid=3044>.

8. Alchin, Linda. "Spanish Conquistadors." *Elizabethan Era*. N.p., 16 May 2012. Web. <http://www.elizabethan-era.org.uk/spanish-conquistadors.htm>.

9. Mikkelson, David. "Morgan Freeman on Black History Month." *Snopes*. N.p., 01 Mar. 2015. Web.

10. Fox News Staff, and Associated Press. "Georgetown University to give slave descendants priority for admission." *Fox News*. FOX News Network, 01 Sept. 2016. Web.

11. Shyong, Frank. "For Asian Americans, a changing landscape on college admissions." *Los Angeles Times*. Los Angeles Times, 21 Feb. 2015. Web.

12. Slater, Dan. "Does Affirmative Action Do What It Should?" *The New York Times*. The New York Times, 16 Mar. 2013. Web.

13. "The model minority is losing patience." *The Economist*. The Economist Newspaper, 03 Oct. 2015. Web.

14. "Population estimates, July 1, 2015, (V2015)." *US Census Bureau*. N.p., n.d. Web.

## Corporate Giants & the One-Percent

1. Sahadi, Jeanne. "The richest 10% hold 76% of wealth." *CNNMoney*. Cable News Network, 18 Aug. 2016. Web.

2. Kane, Libby. "Most of the world's billionaires didn't inherit their wealth - they earned it." *Business Insider*. Business Insider, 16 Apr. 2015. Web.

3. Harjani, Ansuya. "How much do the ultra-rich give to charity?" *CNBC*. CNBC, 06 Oct. 2014. Web.

4. Smith, Jacquelyn. "America's Most Generous Companies." *Forbes*. Forbes Magazine, 16 July 2013. Web.

5. Greenberg, Scott. "Summary of the Latest Federal Income Tax Data, 2015 Update." *Tax Foundation*. Tax Foundation, 19 Nov. 2015. Web.

6. Hodge, Scott. "News To Obama: The OECD Says the United States Has the Most Progressive Tax System." *Tax Foundation*. Tax Foundation, 29 Oct. 2008. Web.

7. Sargent, Greg. "Bernie Sanders calls for downward 'transfer' of wealth of top one percent." *The Washington Post*. WP Company, 26 May 2015. Web.

8. Edsall, Thomas B. "How Did the Democrats Become Favorites of the Rich?" *The New York Times*. The New York Times, 07 Oct. 2015. Web.

9. Savchuk, Katia. "Wealthy Americans Are Giving Less Of Their Incomes To Charity, While Poor Are Donating More." *Forbes*. Forbes Magazine, 06 Oct. 2014. Web.

10. Marte, Jonnelle. "How the super rich invest their money." *The Washington Post*. WP Company, 17 June 2015. Web.

11. Borzykowski, Bryan. "BBC - Capital - Why the rich stay rich: they don't invest like the rest." *BBC News*. BBC, 02 May 2014. Web.

12. Bell, Kay. "Capital gains tax: Your income helps determine what you pay." *Bankrate*. Bankrate, 21 Mar. 2017. Web.

13. Block, David, and William McBride. "Why Capital Gains are taxed at a Lower Rate." *Tax Foundation*. Tax Foundation, 16 Jan. 2017. Web.

14. Sahadi , Jeanne. "Taxing the rich: The record under Obama." *CNNMoney*. Cable News Network, 30 Jan. 2015. Web.

15. Snyder, Michael. "The 20 Craziest Things The U.S. Government Wastes Money On." *Business Insider*. Business Insider, 22 Dec. 2010. Web.

## Educational Collapse

1. "The Hitler Youth." *Holocaust Education & Archive Research Team*. N.p., n.d. Web. <http://www.holocaustresearchproject.org/holoprelude/hitleryouth.html>.

2. Mark. "Posts about education on Ranking America." *Ranking America*. N.p., 06 Jan. 2015. Web.

&lt;https://rankingamerica.wordpress.com/category/education/&gt;.

3. Lynch, Matthew. "10 Reasons the U.S. Education System Is Failing." *Education Week - Education Futures: Emerging Trends in K-12.* N.p., 29 Aug. 2015. Web.

4. Lattier, Daniel. "The Real Problem with American Education?" *Intellectual Takeout.* N.p., 25 Oct. 2016. Web.

5. Layton, Lyndsey. "Study says standardized testing is overwhelming nation's public schools." *The Washington Post.* WP Company, 24 Oct. 2015. Web.

6. "Everybody is a Genius. But If You Judge a Fish by Its Ability to Climb a Tree, It Will Live Its Whole Life Believing that It is Stupid." *Quote Investigator.* N.p., 06 Apr. 2013. Web. &lt;http://quoteinvestigator.com/2013/04/06/fish-climb/&gt;.

7. Chen, Grace. "10 Major Challenges Facing Public Schools." *PublicSchoolReview.com.* N.p., 20 Apr. 2017. Web.

8. Engel, Pamela. "This May Be The Biggest Problem With America's 'Common Core' Education Standards." *Business Insider.* Business Insider, 04 July 2014. Web.

9. Burk, Henry W. "States' Taxpayers Left to Pay for Common Core." *Education News.* N.p., 26 Jan. 2014. Web.

10. Strauss, Valerie. "Eight problems with Common Core Standards." *The Washington Post.* WP Company, 21 Aug. 2012. Web.

11. Edwards, Halle. "How Long is the ACT? | ACT Expert Guide." *PrepScholar.* N.p., 06 Feb. 2015. Web.

12. Edwards, Halle. "Expert Guide: How Long Is the SAT?" *PrepScholar*. N.p., 05 Feb. 2015. Web.

13. Hernández, Javier C. "Common Core, in 9-Year-Old Eyes." *The New York Times*. The New York Times, 14 June 2014. Web.

## International Deterioration

1. "Ukraine conflict: Deadly flare-up in east." *BBC News*. BBC, 30 Jan. 2017. Web.

2. Tancredi, Antonello. "The Russian annexation of the Crimea: questions relating to the use of force." *QIL QDI*. N.p., 11 May 2014. Web.

3. "Nuclear Weapons: Who Has What at a Glance." *Arms Control Association*. N.p., 07 Apr. 2017. Web. <https://www.armscontrol.org/factsheets/Nuclearweaponswhohaswhat>.

4. Sanger, David E. "Iran Sticks to Terms of Nuclear Deal, but Defies the U.S. in Other Ways." *The New York Times*. The New York Times, 13 July 2016. Web.

5. Drury, Flora. "Revealed - how the threat of ISIS is spreading: Extremist group has DOUBLED the land it controls in just a few months despite more than 800 coalition airstrikes ." *Daily Mail Online*. Associated Newspapers, 17 Jan. 2015. Web.

6. Fantz, Ashley. "War on ISIS: Who's doing what?" *CNN*. Cable News Network, 27 Nov. 2015. Web.

7. Parsons, Christi, and W.J. Hennigan. "President Obama, who hoped to sow peace, instead led the nation in war." *Los Angeles Times*. Los Angeles Times, 13 Jan. 2017. Web.

8. Browne, Ryan. "State Department report finds Iran is top state sponsor of terror." *CNN*. Cable News Network, 02 June 2016. Web.

9. "The Current Situation in Libya." *United States Institute of Peace*. N.p., 16 May 2016. Web.

10. "Trump responds to sanctions against Russia, says it's time to 'move on'" *Fox News*. FOX News Network, 29 Dec. 2016. Web.

11. Johnson, Kevin. "FBI accepts CIA conclusion that Russians hacked to help Trump." *USA Today*. Gannett Satellite Information Network, 16 Dec. 2016. Web.

12. Wachtel, Jonathan. "UN resolution is one of dozens of rebukes against Israel in 2016." *Fox News*. FOX News Network, 27 Dec. 2016. Web.

13. Dilanian, Ken. "New Cold War? Russia, U.S. Relations At Lowest Point Since 1970s." *NBCNews.com*. NBCUniversal News Group, 05 Oct. 2016. Web.

14. Tomlinson, Lucas, and Jennifer Griffin. "Iran tests ballistic missile in defiance of UN resolution, US officials say." *Fox News*. FOX News Network, 30 Jan. 2017. Web.

15. Diamond, Jeremy. "House charges Obama broke law in Bowe Bergdahl swap." *CNN*. Cable News Network, 10 Dec. 2015. Web.

16. Rasmussen, Sune Engel. "Afghanistan funds abusive militias as US military 'ignores' situation, officials say." *The Guardian*. Guardian News and Media, 26 Dec. 2016. Web.

17. Kaplan, Rebecca. "ISIS a bigger threat than pre-9/11 al Qaeda?" *CBS News*. CBS Interactive, 11 Aug. 2014. Web.

18. Takala, Rudy. "CIA: ISIS now bigger than al Qaeda at its height." *Washington Examiner*. N.p., 16 June 2016. Web.

19. "FOCUS ON: PEARL HARBOR:." *The National WWII Museum New Orleans*. N.p., n.d. Web <http://www.nationalww2museum.org/see-hear/collections/focus-on/pearl-harbor.html?gclid=Cj0KEQiAiMHEBRC034nx2ImB1J0BEiQA-r7ctvV9MhyPYBw_HnWi2Uz-8dvxbcAr0sPaykVGSd80RdcaAiCV8P8HAQ%3Freferrer>.

20. History.com Staff. "Bombing of Hiroshima and Nagasaki." *History.com*. A&E Television Networks, n.d. Web.

21. "Isoroku Yamamoto Quotes." *BrainyQuote*. Xplore, n.d. Web.

## The Abandonment of Morality

1. Darcy, Oliver. "Jay Z repeatedly drops n-word, f-bomb during concert for Hillary Clinton." *Business Insider*. Business Insider, 04 Nov. 2016. Web.

2. Peoples, Glenn. "How, and How Much, America Listens Have Been Measured for the First Time." *Billboard*. N.p., 18 June 2014. Web.

3. Parker-Pope, Tara. "Under the Influence of...Music?" *The New York Times*. The New York Times, 05 Feb. 2008. Web.

4. Howard, Jacqueline. "STD rates reach record high in United States." *CNN*. Cable News Network, 20 Oct. 2016. Web.

5. Metcalfe, Luke. "Countries Compared by Health > Teenage pregnancy. International Statistics." *NationMaster.com*. NationMaster, n.d. Web.

6. "Child Sexual Abuse Statistics." *Darkness to Light*. N.p., n.d. Web. <http://www.d2l.org/the-issue/statistics/>.

7. Mikkelson, David. "Company Releases 'Child Love Dolls' to Stop Pedophiles." *Snopes.com*. N.p., 26 Apr. 2015. Web.

8. Warren, Amber. "Sex Offenders Have Shockingly Short Sentences." *Crime Wire*. Crimewire, 15 Sept. 2016. Web.

9. "Kyle Carpenter (@chiksdigscars)." *Twitter*. Twitter, n.d. Web. <https://twitter.com/chiksdigscars>.

10. "Danielle Bregoli (@TheBhadBhabie)." *Twitter*. Twitter, n.d. Web. <https://twitter.com/TheBhadBhabie>.

11. Kircher, Madison Malone. "A Brief History of 'Cash Me Outside, Howbow Dah?'" *Select All*. Nymag, 2 Feb. 2017. Web.

12. Manuel, Adam. "10 Celebs Who Don't Deserve Their Fame And Fortune." *TheRichest*. N.p., 18 Dec. 2015. Web.

13. Brown, Emma. "Meet the teen who just won $150,000 for inventing a device to diagnose lung disease." *The Washington Post*. WP Company, 16 Mar. 2016. Web.

14. Russon, Mary-Ann. "3D-Printed Skull Replacement Transplant a World First for Netherlands Patient." *International Business Times UK*. N.p., 26 Mar. 2014. Web.

15. Henderson, Barney, and David Lawler. "Donald Trump: the 22 wildest moments of his 2016 presidential election campaign - so far." *The Telegraph*. Telegraph Media Group, 31 Aug. 2016. Web.

16. Singman, Brooke. "Trump honors widow of fallen US Navy SEAL in emotional moment." *Fox News*. FOX News Network, 28 Feb. 2017. Web.

17. Yahr, Emily. "SNL writer suspended for Barron Trump tweet, writes apology: 'It was incxcusable'." *The Washington Post*. WP Company, 24 Jan. 2017. Web.

18. "'Keep Fighting': Hillary Urges 'Resistance and Persistence' in Message to DNC." *Fox News*. FOX News Network, 24 Feb. 2017. Web.

19. Livingston, Gretchen. "Fewer than half of U.S. kids today live in a 'traditional' family." *Pew Research Center*. N.p., 22 Dec. 2014. Web.

## Capitalism versus Socialism

1. "Vladimir Lenin Quotes." *BrainyQuote*. Xplore, n.d. Web. <https://www.brainyquote.com/quotes/authors/v/vladimir_leni n.html>.

2. Ushistory.org. "Comparing Economic Systems." *American Government Online Textbook*. Independence Hall Association, n.d. Web.

3. Recluse, Alias. "The basic principles of Marxism - Critique Sociale." *Libcom.org*. N.p., 23 Dec. 2013. Web.

4.  Spalding, Roger. "The Communist Manifesto." *History Today*. N.p., n.d. Web.

5.  "HISTORY OF CAPITALISM." *History World*. N.p., n.d. Web. <http://www.historyworld.net/wrldhis/PlainTextHistories.asp?historyid=aa49>.

6.  Welch, William. "Adam Smith: Capitalism's Founding Father." *Vision.org*. N.p., n.d. Web.

7.  Rampell, Catherine. "Opinion | Millennials have a higher opinion of socialism than of capitalism." *The Washington Post*. WP Company, 05 Feb. 2016. Web.

8.  Dearden, Lizzie. "Berlin Wall: What you need to know about the barrier that divided East and West." *The Independent*. Independent Digital News and Media, 08 Nov. 2014. Web.

9.  "Karl Marx Quotes." *BrainyQuote*. Xplore, n.d. Web. <https://www.brainyquote.com/search_results.html?q=karl%2Bmarx%2Bquotes>.

10. "The Economic Collapse of the Soviet Union." *Applet-magic.com*. San José State University Department of Economics, n.d. Web.

11. Fein, Esther B. "Soviet Openness Brings Poverty Out of the Shadows." *The New York Times*. The New York Times, 29 Jan. 1989. Web.

12. Newman, Rick. "Here's How Lousy Life Is in North Korea." *U.S. News & World Report*. U.S. News & World Report, 12 Apr. 2013. Web.

13. "The World Factbook." *Central Intelligence Agency*. Central Intelligence Agency, n.d. Web.

&lt;https://www.cia.gov/library/publications/the-world-factbook/fields/2046.html&gt;.

14. Mcneil, Donald G. "Life Span of South Korean Women Is Headed Toward 90." *The New York Times*. The New York Times, 27 Feb. 2017. Web.

15. "Life expectancy at birth, total (years)." *The World Bank*. N.p., n.d. Web. &lt;http://data.worldbank.org/indicator/SP.DYN.LE00.IN&gt;.

16. Sahadi, Jeanne. "Top income tax rate: How U.S. really compares." *CNNMoney*. Cable News Network, 1 Apr. 2013. Web.

17. Hegseth, Pete. "Single-Payer Health Care: America Already Has It." *PragerU*. N.p., 10 Apr. 2017. Web.

18. Bronstein, Scott. "Hospital delays are killing America's war veterans." *CNN*. Cable News Network, 20 Nov. 2013. Web.

19. Crowder, Steven. "Democratic Socialism is Still Socialism." *PragerU*. N.p., 31 Oct. 2016. Web.

20. Davis, Karen, Kristof Stremikis, David Squires, and Cathy Schoen. "How the U.S. Health Care System Compares Internationally." *The Commonwealth Fund*. N.p., 16 June 2014. Web.

21. Druzin, Randi. "Crossing the Border for Care." *U.S. News & World Report*. U.S. News & World Report, 03 Aug. 2016. Web.

22. Graham, John R. ""Free" Canadian Health Care At $12,000 Per Family." *Health Policy Blog RSS*. National Center for Policy Analysis, 21 Aug. 2015. Web.

23. "Angela Merkel approves Germany's first minimum wage." *BBC News*. BBC, 02 Apr. 2014. Web.

24. Gobry, Pascal-Emmanuel . "Attention Bernie Sanders: Europe gave up on its socialist paradise years ago." *The Week*. N.p., 22 Jan. 2016. Web.

25. May, Paul. "Canada's sanctuary for migrants is built on a strict immigration policy." *Los Angeles Times*. Los Angeles Times, 28 Dec. 2016. Web.

26. Prager, Dennis. "Socialism Makes People Selfish." *PragerU*. N.p., 18 July 2016. Web.

## Feminism: Is it Necessary?

1. Sommers, Christina. "There Is No Gender Wage Gap." *PragerU*. N.p., 06 Mar. 2017. Web.

2. Trister, Sarah. "Women's Rights in the Middle East and North Africa: Supporting the Fight for Freedom and Equality." *The Huffington Post*. TheHuffingtonPost.com, 10 Mar. 2010. Web.

3. "Women's Rights in Iran." *Human Rights Watch*. N.p., 28 Oct. 2015. Web.

4. "Saudi Arabia's women vote in election for first time." *BBC News*. BBC, 12 Dec. 2015. Web.

5. "The Equal Pay Act of 1963." *U.S. Equal Employment Opportunity Commission*. N.p., n.d. Web. <https://www.eeoc.gov/laws/statutes/epa.cfm>.

6. Perry, Mark J. "'Equal Pay Day' this year was April 12 -- the next 'Equal Occupational Fatality Day' will be on February 19, 2027." *AEIdeas*. AEI, 16 Dec. 2016. Web.

7. "Suicide Statistics." *American Foundation for Suicide Prevention*. N.p., n.d. Web. <https://afsp.org/about-suicide/suicide-statistics/>.

8. "Crime in the United States 2010 - Expanded Homicide Data." *FBI: UCR*. Federal Bureau of Investigation, 26 July 2011. Web.

9. "Latest U.S. Custody and Child Support Data." *Dalrock*. N.p., 15 Aug. 2011. Web.

10. "Deaths from the War in Iraq." *ProCon.org*. N.p., 28 Oct. 2013. Web.

11. Riddell, Kelly. "Pro-life women banned from anti-Trump Women's March on Washington." *The Washington Times*. The Washington Times, 17 Jan. 2017. Web.

12. Barber, Nigel. "Sexual Wiring of Women's Breasts." *Psychology Today*. Sussex Publishers, 07 May 2013. Web.

13. Bahadur, Nina. "'Femvertising' Ads Are Empowering Women -- And Making Money For Brands." *The Huffington Post*. TheHuffingtonPost.com, 02 Oct. 2014. Web.

## Our Future

1. CNN Staff. "At the Brandenburg Gate." *CNN*. Cable News Network, n.d. Web. <http://www.cnn.com/SPECIALS/2004/reagan/stories/speech.archive/brandenburg.html>.